Reasonable Disagreement

T0347421

Politics and Policy in American Institutions
Volume 2
Garland Reference Library of Social Science
Volume 1157

Politics and Policy in American Institutions

Steven A. Shull, *Series Editor*

PRESIDENTS AS CANDIDATES
Inside the White House
for the Presidential Campaign
Kathryn Dunn Tenpas

REASONABLE DISAGREEMENT
Two U.S. Senators and
the Choices They Make
Karl A. Lamb

Reasonable Disagreement

Two U.S. Senators and the Choices They Make

Karl A. Lamb

Routledge
Taylor & Francis Group

NEW YORK AND LONDON

Also by Karl A. Lamb

The Guardians: *Leadership Values and the American Tradition*
As Orange Goes: *Twelve California Families and the Future of American Politics*
The People, Maybe
Campaign Decision-Making: *The Presidential Election of 1964*
    (with Paul A. Smith)
Congress: Politics and Practice (with Norman C. Thomas)
Apportionment and Representative Institutions: *The Michigan Experience*
    (with William J. Pierce and John P. White)

First published 1998 by Garland Publishing, Inc.

This edition published 2013 by Routledge
711 Third Avenue, New York, NY 10017
2 Park Square, Milton Park, Abingdon, Oxon OX14 4RN

Routledge is an imprint of the Taylor & Francis Group, an informa business

Copyright © 1998 by Karl A. Lamb

Library of Congress Cataloging-in-Publication Data

Lamb, Karl A.
        Reasonable disagreement : two U.S. Senators and the choices they
    make / Karl A. Lamb
            p.   cm. — (Politics and policy in American institutions ;
    v. 2. Garland reference library of social science ; v. 1157)
        Includes bibliographical references and index.
        ISBN 0-8153-2801-X (alk. paper). — ISBN 0–8153–2802–8
    (pbk. : alk. paper)
        1. Sarbanes, Paul—Political and social views.   2. Lugar,
    Richard—Political and social views.   3. Legislators—United States—
    Biography.   4. United States.   Congress.   Senate—Biography.
    5. United States—Politics and government—1945–1989.   6. United
    States—Politics and government—1989–   7. Political culture—
    Indiana.   8. Political culture—Maryland.   I. Title.   II. Series:
    Garland reference library of social science. Politics and policy in
    American institutions ; v. 2.   III. Series: Garland reference library of
    social science ; v. 1157.
    E840.6.L36   1998
    328.73'092'2—dc21   98-19160
                                                                                CIP

Cover: Senators Paul Sarbanes *(left)* and Richard Lugar *(right)*.
Cover Design: Bill Brown Design

Dedicated to the memory of
Lawrence Lamb
1901–1994

CONTENTS

ACKNOWLEDGMENTS

This project would have been impossible without the cooperation and interest of the principals, Paul Sarbanes and Dick Lugar. I have described my twenty years of conversations with them in chapter 1. Further thanks are due to all those who have granted interviews over the years—members of the senators' families, congressional staff members, party officials, people I talked to at campaign rallies. If known, their names are recorded in the notes, although my gratitude is only expressed here.

The project received financial support at various times from the Earhart Foundation, the Research Committee of the University of California, Santa Cruz, Faculty Senate, and from the Naval Academy Research Council. The Naval Academy also provided sabbatical leave for the spring semester of 1992. My thanks to John Fitzgerald and Colonel Mike Hagee, USMC, for endorsing the application, and to Bob Shapiro for approving it.

Mrs. Barbara Breeden of the Nimitz Library, U.S. Naval Academy, has been cheerfully helpful in tracing books and documents. For taking a critical interest in the project, I thank my former colleague, Professor John Schaar of Santa Cruz, and my present one, Professor Stephen Frantzich of the Naval Academy. Under the guidance of the Anne Arundel County high schools' mentorship program, Tasha Dunn served ably as my research assistant during the summer of 1995.

I am honored that this volume will help initiate the new series in public policy and American institutions edited by Steve Shull. I thank him for insisting on a clearer focus for the book, while he maintained an inspiring enthusiasm for its subject. David Estrin of Garland Publishing handled logistics problems with jovial good humor and notable efficiency, as well as sustained enthusiasm for the book. Chuck Bartelt of Garland persuaded very different computer programs to make common cause, and Natalie Bowen copy edited the manuscript sensitively, with near total consistency.

My greatest debt is to Sally, my wife, for putting up with the writing of yet another book. She has reviewed drafts of every chapter and gently insisted that I say what I mean. Our daughter, Amy, reviewed a draft of the final chapter while flying to Seattle and phoned back her helpful critique.

I owe much to the people mentioned here for any virtues the book may contain. Much as I may wish it otherwise, I cannot hold them responsible for its flaws.

CHAPTER 1

Two Senators and Their Disagreements

In the final decade of the twentieth century, how does America go to war? Our eighteenth-century founders decreed that such decisions be made jointly by the president, who is commander-in-chief of the military forces, and Congress, the people's elected representatives. Thus, in the Constitution, while the president commands the resources to make war, only Congress can "declare" war. In the eighteenth century, wars were the playgrounds of kings, often fought by mercenaries hired in foreign lands. After Napoleon, serious wars engaged entire national populations, and two of them involved most of the world. Congress has declared war five times in U.S. history; American forces have fought in several hundred conflicts—ranging from a raid on the Barbary pirates to the Korean "police action"—without the benefit of a declaration by Congress, which nevertheless continued to pay the bills.

Soon after Iraq invaded Kuwait on August 2, 1990, President Bush declared that the aggression "must not stand." He assembled a coalition of nations to oppose Saddam Hussein, and he directed an immediate deployment of American forces to the Persian Gulf. But he did not consult Congress, and Congress did not complain. It did not seem right for the 250 million people of the United States to declare war on the 12 million souls of Iraq, no matter how much of the world's oil Saddam Hussein proposed to control. A Congressional election campaign was going on, and a new, controversial issue might threaten the incumbents' reelection.

Two days after the election, President Bush announced the doubling of the American troop commitment in the Gulf region from

200,000 to 400,000, signaling the change from a defensive to an offensive posture. Indiana Republican senator Richard G. Lugar and Senate minority leader Robert Dole publicly recommended a special session of Congress to debate the issue. President Bush would not pursue a special session when Senator Dole could not guarantee that a resolution of support would pass in the Senate. "Privately, Lugar was telling Bush it would be better to find out now whether he lacked the congressional support, rather than later."[1]

The Democratic position was dramatized in November hearings of the Senate Armed Services and Foreign Relations Committees. Witnesses deplored the eagerness of the Bush administration to abandon economic sanctions, arguing that the embargo would be effective if left in place for twelve to eighteen months. Maryland senator Paul S. Sarbanes was a determined spokesman for this liberal Democratic position, which was partly based on the presumed lessons of Vietnam.

In early December, at the request of the United States, the United Nations authorized member nations to use force if Iraq did not leave Kuwait by January 15, 1991. Saddam Hussein suddenly agreed to release the foreign nationals he had been holding hostage. Senator Dole claimed that Iraq's concession vindicated President Bush's strategy of forcing Hussein's hand. Senator Sarbanes replied that this objective of American policy had been achieved without bloodshed; sanctions could succeed.[2]

In a quasi-debate on television with Richard Lugar, Paul Sarbanes argued that the administration had set the nation on a course for war, without giving sanctions a chance. Lugar replied that Saddam Hussein would be unmoved even if sanctions brought starvation to his people, but the dictator would understand force. When Lugar again called for an immediate special session of Congress, Sarbanes questioned the legitimacy of the lame duck Congress. He said that the new Congress, with a 10 percent change in personnel, would be in closer touch with the American people.[3]

The new Congress convened on schedule. Then President Bush asked Congress to support the use of American ground forces, and the Senate launched three days of debate which climaxed on Saturday, January 12. One by one, senators rose either to express misgivings about the rush to war or to announce regretfully that the alternatives to combat had been exhausted.

Senator Sarbanes charged that the administration's growing impatience with economic sanctions had made it "the prisoner of its own rhetoric, with American options and [the American] timetable thereby severely constricted."[4] Sarbanes first quoted from, then inserted into the

Congressional Record, the full testimony of former Joint Chiefs chairman Admiral William J. Crowe and other experts who claimed that economic sanctions would eventually be effective. He concluded,

> The question is not between countenancing or tolerating Saddam Hussein's aggression on the one hand and going to war on the other. There is another alternative, and the other alternative is . . . to make him and Iraq pay a very high price for what they have done . . . [W]e cannot, in good conscience and good faith, say now to any family that loses a member in a military conflict that every avenue to achieve a peaceful resolution was explored.

Some senators supporting Bush's action claimed that congressional approval would demonstrate the seriousness of the American people to Saddam Hussein, and he would back down. Senator Lugar did not accept this wishful assumption. His statement emphasized the need for American credibility in international relations.

> We are a reluctant superpower and many Americans will argue that we should not be involved all over the world in maintaining peace and advancing our ideals . . . Our votes today express our determination to prevail. The moment of accountability has come. I have supported President Bush as he has sought peace in international law, and I will support his request that he be authorized to use military force.

After debate was concluded, the Senate approved military action by 52 to 47. Only ten Democrats voted for the resolution, but they assured its victory. Republican Lugar voted for the resolution, while Democrat Sarbanes rejected it. The resolution was then approved by the House of Representatives and welcomed by President Bush.

This debate was better attended by Senate members than most discussions on the Senate floor. The gravity of its subject caused emotions to run high and drew more than the usual attention from the media and the public. Yet the discussion remained reasonable. Passionate convictions were expressed verbally, not physically. All senators had their say, and the final votes by both houses of Congress answered the question definitively: by a slender margin, Congress supported President Bush's determination to launch the attack soon labeled Desert Storm.

Reasonable disagreement that leads to compromise and sometimes raucous, more often meandering, debate that usually concludes decisively are hallmarks of Senate business. But even when disagreements are rea-

sonable, many onlookers are distressed. The inability of democratic institutions to act harmoniously disturbs a public that is attached to an abstract and unrealistic vision of democracy. Careful opinion research
shows that voters are upset by features of Congress usually listed as features of democracy—disagreement, long-windedness, the recognition of
organized pressure groups, and compromise.[5]

Senators Paul Sarbanes and Richard Lugar were on opposite sides of
the Desert Storm debate, as they have been for most major issues decided
during the two decades they have served together in the United States
Senate. These two men represent the Senate mainstream, the members of
the upper chamber who accomplish its business. The Edward Kennedys
and the Jesse Helmses of the Senate make news by vehemently expressing
opinions contrary to those of many colleagues—and of each other. The
echoes of such disputes reach the general public, who complain that the
politicians favor extremes and neglect the middle ground.[6] The public
seems to want the best of all worlds: legislators who avoid extreme positions to achieve compromise, while standing firmly on principle; members of Congress who are sensitive to constituent desires but do not bend
in the breeze of public opinion.

Senators like Sarbanes and Lugar focus more on achieving legislation
than on gaining personal publicity from the process. Sarbanes has carefully chosen to develop influence as an insider and neglects the senatorial
games that attract media attention. Taking advantage of the fact that
Maryland surrounds the District of Columbia on three sides, Sarbanes
has maintained an ordinary private life, along with his family, living in
Baltimore. Lugar emerged from involvement in Senate affairs (and frequent appearance to discuss foreign policy on Sunday morning talk
shows) to seek the 1996 Republican presidential nomination. The reporters, who are the most important audience in the early primary contests,
criticized the Indiana senator for being too reasonable, and hence too
dull, to win convention delegates. The qualities that make him an effective senator did not serve him well in the quest for a national following,
but he returned to the senatorial life in good spirits.

Paul Sarbanes has been among the most liberal of liberal Democratic senators since entering the Senate in 1977. Richard Lugar was as
conservative a Republican as could be found in the Senate of the late
1970s. But his party has changed, taking a conservative stance on social
issues that were not even part of public discourse twenty years ago.
Some Republicans who entered the Senate long after Lugar consider
him a "moderate." The immoderate connotation of the label is to sug-

gest a person who is essentially an outsider in the new Republican party.

Paul Sarbanes and Dick Lugar have known each other since 1954, when they met as members of the Rhodes Scholars' sailing party, going to take up residence in Oxford. Remarkable similarities in their life stories make the differences stand out sharply. The two future senators were children of the Great Depression who were shielded by their families from its most soul-destroying aspects. They are about the same age (Sarbanes was born almost exactly ten months after Lugar); both were firstborn sons; their educations are comparable; both take religion seriously; and the timing of changes in their careers has been much alike. Their equal Senate seniority has given them neighboring office suites in the marble temple of the Hart Senate Office Building (although the offices are entered from separate corridors). Despite these similarities, they seem destined to oppose one another on public issues. The causes they have championed as senators, like their voting records, have been in striking contrast for two decades. The story of those two decades is a tale of partisanship, political change, and reasonable disagreement. This book examines their frequent disagreements and finds in aspects of their life experiences reasons why they take particular positions and cast specific votes.

Paul Sarbanes and Richard Lugar are reasonable men, able and distinguished. Though they disagree on most major issues, neither loses patience with the other, because both understand the reasons for disagreement. Their concurrent careers in the Senate have included the presidencies of Jimmy Carter, Ronald Reagan, George Bush, and Bill Clinton. Lugar and Sarbanes have been caught up in the dynamics of the presidential–congressional relationship. Both have been members of the Foreign Relations Committee for most of that time, putting them at the center of the special constitutional role the Senate plays in the conduct of foreign relations.

The Research Task

The combination of political analysis and biographical detail reported here depends on access to the two subjects over an extended period of time. I have imposed my research interests on my two Oxford classmates sporadically for twenty years. I first interviewed them in 1977, in connection with a broader study. The present research was first conceived in 1980. During the campaign period of 1982, when both were running for second terms in the Senate, I visited Indiana and Maryland, recording interviews with them, their political associates, friends, and families. I was a participant-observer at campaign events. Further interviews were conducted in 1983.

In 1985, I left the University of California, Santa Cruz, to undertake administrative responsibilities at the U.S. Naval Academy, becoming a constituent of Paul Sarbanes. This meant laying aside the study of two senators, even as I moved to a city thirty miles from the Capitol building where they work. I took up the project again in 1990 and have recorded interviews with the two senators periodically while keeping in touch with their staffs. This book thus is based on two decades of sporadic research, and it was made possible by the patience of its two subjects, who somehow found time to talk about their activities, even when no book appeared to justify my curiosity.

In the vast explosion of scholarship focused on the Congress in the last three decades, the House of Representatives has received more attention than the Senate. This is probably because the House offers greater numbers, supplying the grist for quantitative studies. It is also because a scholar who wins the confidence of a member of the House is able to promise anonymity in the resulting publication. This is not so easy in the Senate, for each state has but two senators; the reader can too easily penetrate whatever disguise the writer contrives. This book is written in the belief that real senators should be identified by name.

The Determinants of Senatorial Action

Sarbanes and Lugar seem destined to disagree. While fate or destiny may explain causes in literature, it will not suffice in social science. Any explanation of why legislators act as they do must begin with a theory about the causes of, or influences upon, those actions. It necessarily begins by asking, what kind of person is the legislator?

Responding to the critics' claim that legislators are the passive instruments of their campaign contributors, former senator Warren Rudman of New Hampshire has posed and answered the relevant question.

> Who are we when we're elected to the Senate? . . . We are men and women. We are not bland, neutral, blank-slate people who never suffered, and never were happy. You tend to be influenced by the sum total of life's experiences.[7]

While Senator Rudman's comment bears the ring of truth, the "sum total of life's experiences" too easily becomes a catchall when discussing causality. The sum total must be broken into its component parts to allow analysis. Following the lead of fellow political scientists, I have established six categories of influence to help compare the lives of Senators Lugar and Sarbanes.[8]

More than some other occupations, the work of a legislator involves making choices. An element of legislative skill is the ability to frame questions that can be answered "aye" or "nay." The legislator's approach to serving the constituency, shaping legislation in committee, seeking public support through the media, or lobbying colleagues for a particular bill, all require choices which culminate when the institution makes its choice through voting on the Senate floor. *Choice* is the senatorial action to be explained.

Two kinds of influence are at work. The first is external, such as constituency pressure or the president's preference. The second is personal and internal: the senator's personality or policy goals. These types are further divided into background influences which the senator hardly feels at the time of decision, because they have been so completely internalized, and influences which surge to the foreground and are consciously considered at the point of decision. The six influences to be examined in the lives of Dick Lugar and Paul Sarbanes are shown in Table 1–1.

These influences are numbered in the order in which they become significant in the senator's life. The first is personality, which is succinctly defined as "the set of individually evolved characteristic patterns of behavior which determine daily functioning on both conscious and unconscious levels."[9] Personality most nearly matches what Barber calls "character" in his study of presidents. It is rooted in the individual's childhood but modified by later experiences. In part, personality is formed by the

TABLE 1–1

Influences on Senatorial Choice

	Developed early in life	Considered consciously
Personal (internalized)	1. Personality 2. Ideology	5. Policy preference
External	3. Constituency 4. Party	6. Political context

individual's expectations of, and relationship with, the wider world. For example, it is significant that both Sarbanes and Lugar are firstborn sons who luxuriated in the undivided attention of their parents.

Ideology is the label given to that set of connected beliefs that forms the individual's understanding of the social world, allowing him or her to assimilate diverse new stimuli. The dominant ideology of a nation usually justifies the attitudes and activities of that country's most influential economic, political, or religious groups. The word's connotation suggests that an ideology may supply an incomplete or biased view of reality. American politicians tend to use "philosophy" as the label for an individual's interconnected political beliefs. In common usage, mainstream American ideologies are divided into liberal and conservative, with extremes of either persuasion called "radical."

An individual's ideology (Barber's "world view") is mightily influenced by the ideas and experiences of adolescence, but it may not coalesce into a kind of lifetime goal or ambition until early adulthood. Dick Lugar was a staunch conservative and Paul Sarbanes an avid liberal when they completed high school, and their beliefs were reinforced in college. But their years as Rhodes Scholars encouraged them to aim toward electoral politics.

Both personality and ideology are thoroughly internalized. They are so well established that the individual is seldom conscious of their influence at the time of making a choice. Yet influences that are clearly external may have such an impact over time that they blend with ideology and become background considerations at the point of choice, rather than considerations to be constantly weighed.

The relationship between the representative and the constituency is a continuing one and is central to the politician's craft. The way that relationship is established and maintained depends on the representative's personality and the nature of the apprenticeship in which the politician's craft was learned and perfected. Before entering the Senate, Richard Lugar served as mayor of Indianapolis. He was recruited for the candidacy by the Republican organization. In contrast, Paul Sarbanes was elected to the Maryland legislature as a reform candidate, and he ran for the U.S. House of Representatives against the advice of party veterans.

The senator's constituency, or groups within it, are usually portrayed as the most important influence on senatorial actions, because the constituency controls the senator's future through the power to deny reelection. Of course, senators make every effort to determine constituency opinion. But most senators represent the states where they were born, or at least grew up, where they spent the majority of their years before coming to Washington. Products of a particular political culture, they have experienced both the area's shortages and its surpluses. They come to feel as if they were born knowing what their constituents need. The "law of anticipated reaction" operates. The senator is sure he knows what the voters of his state would want, if they were aware that the question had arisen. Thus the consideration of constituency has already taken place, in a sense, when the point of choice is reached.

Both Senator Lugar and Senator Sarbanes represent the states they were born in and returned to after completing their educations. Both follow opinion polling in their home states and encourage their parties to commission further polls. Their offices are organized to report the opinions of visitors, callers, letter writers, and the senders of e-mail. But neither senator expresses uncertainty about knowing what his constituents want.

Both the relationship with constituents and the interactions of the representative with his or her colleagues in the process of governing are powerfully mediated by the representative's membership in a political party. Many constituents will judge the representative by the party label. Some of the representative's votes will be influenced by concerns for party advantage. And whatever ambitions for higher office the representative entertains will be sought in the context of party membership.

Lugar and Sarbanes developed party identities as children which became part of their self-image. Paul Sarbanes, the son of Greek immigrants, grew up in a Democratic household and has always been a Democrat; Dick Lugar followed several generations of his family into the GOP. The uniformed portrait of an ancestor who helped Abraham Lincoln save the Union graced the family home as Dick Lugar was growing up.

Growing into manhood, the two senators experienced different political cultures. Indiana has a strong two-party system, although it has been staunchly Republican in recent presidential elections. Indiana's party organizations retain some characteristics of nineteenth-century patronage–oriented politics. After the party recruited Dick Lugar, the party organization and the mayor formed a symbiotic relationship.

Maryland's parties continued the patronage-focused traditions until they were rocked by a series of scandals in the 1970s. Paul Sarbanes entered the partisan contest as a reform candidate in Baltimore, where office is gained by winning the Democratic primary. His habitual supporters are mainly Democrats, but they form a personal, rather than a party, organization.

These four determinants of senatorial choice (personality, ideology, constituency, and party) are, in this model, relegated to a background position as influences that are well established before the senator confronts the need for a particular choice. Obviously, new claims may be made by the party or the constituency at the time of a specific choice, and the senator will be well aware of them. The four influences converge at the time of choice in favor of a particular alternative. The senator's policy preferences are the end product of the first four influences; in other words, the sum of other determinants mixed together is articulated in the mind as the policy preference. Individuals may not understand how long-forgotten childhood events shaped their understanding of the world, but they are well aware of their own preferences for public policy. In many cases, a legislator will wish to preserve current policy. Preventing policy change may require actions comparable to those needed to bring it about.

The most immediate influence on the choice to be made is the senator's estimate of the political context. This is simply the situation in which the alternatives for choice are posed. One aspect of the political context is related to the senator's progress in a senatorial career, his stage in the "life cycle" of a senator; a freshman senator may have a more solicitous attitude toward constituent opinion than a five-term veteran who has announced his retirement.

Another element of the political context is presidential leadership and activity on the issue concerned. Senators may be—but are not automatically—inclined to support a president of their own party. A third element of the political context is public opinion on the issue concerned, insofar as it has been expressed and measured. An inevitable part of the senator's calculation will concern the amount of influence he feels he can yield on the issue with fellow senators.

At the time of choice, when a lobbyist expects reassurance, or a roll-call vote demands a decision, the senator consciously reviews the political context to determine whether, and how, his or her policy preference can be supported. The other influences culminate in the policy preference; the estimate of the political context determines the strategic route to be followed in achieving or preventing the change.

These broad categories of influence on senatorial behavior are delineated for purposes of analysis, to make manageable the components of "the sum total of life's experiences." The boundaries between the categories are vague, and their impact is overlapping. For example, where does ideology end and partisanship begin? Senators have a clear notion of what their parties stand for, or ought to stand for. This idea informs their policy preferences, and vice versa. Taken together, these six influences provide a theory to guide a search through their parallel biographies for explanations of the two senators' contrasting positions.[10]

Two Senators and the Senate

The trajectories of these two careers in the U.S. Senate—careers that are not yet complete—are rich and varied. The stories of Paul Sarbanes and Dick Lugar provide examples of the contemporary senatorial life cycle which may illuminate the careers of their colleagues. Therefore, this book has a dual subject matter. Its first topic is a quest for the determinants of the contrasting attitudes, actions, and votes of these two remarkably similar men. The second is the Senate itself. To study two of the senators who make the Senate function leads to an understanding of how and why the Senate operates and suggests some reasons for the occasional failures of the institution and of its individual members.

The book is organized according to the theoretical framework set forth here. Chapter 2 concerns formation of the two senators' personalities in infancy and youth and their early political success in high school and college. Chapter 3 deals with the reinforcement of their ideologies and the development of their life ambitions while studying abroad and working for mentors at home. Chapter 4 examines the different political cultures of Maryland and Indiana, describing the roles Sarbanes and Lugar have come to play in them, and compares their Senate performances with those of the other senators from their states during their tenure of office.

The political party is a key element of political culture, and the influence of the party, which begins in youth, is solidified and internalized in the senators' political apprenticeships, the topic of Chapter 5. Chapter 6 illustrates the two senators' implementation of policy choices. It compares their voting records over two decades and describes their choice of committees and their initial legislative initiatives in the Senate. Chapter 7 deals with their adaptations to changing political contexts, such as the elections of Presidents Ronald Reagan and Bill Clinton.

Chapter 8 returns to the constituencies to examine the impact of reelection campaigns on the senators' choices and on the senators themselves. Chapter 9 examines the use Lugar and Sarbanes have made of the freedom given them by the wide margins of repeated reelections. It describes the two senators' quest for leadership positions, which culminated in Dick Lugar's candidacy for the Republican presidential nomination.

Chapter 10 ends the book with a final look at the determinants of senatorial choice, followed by a discussion of lessons these two careers teach about the nature of the Senate. Conclusions are reached about Senate procedures, a new conception of the senatorial life cycle, the movement for term limits, and the need for campaign finance reform.

Notes

1. Bob Woodward, *The Commanders* (New York: Pocket Books, 1991), p. 312.
2. David S. Broder, "Partisan Split Deepens in U.S. Policy Debate," *Washington Post*, December 7, 1990, p. A29.
3. After excerpts were shown from the Senate Foreign Relations Committee hearings, Sarbanes and Lugar were interviewed jointly on the *MacNeil-Lehrer Report* of the Public Broadcasting System, December 5, 1990. Attributions are from a videotape of the broadcast, supplied by Senator Sarbanes' office.
4. All quotations in this chapter from speeches made on the Senate floor are from the *Congressional Record,* January 12, 1991.
5. John R. Hibbing and Elizabeth Theiss-Morse, *Congress As Public Enemy* (Cambridge: Cambridge University Press, 1995), pp. 145–150.
6. Among the vast literature with comparable themes, see E.J. Dionne, Jr., *Why Americans Hate Politics* (New York: Simon and Schuster, 1991) and Alan Ehrenhalt, *The United States of Ambition: Politicians, Power, and the Pursuit of Office* (New York: Times Books, 1991).
7. Quoted in Laura Blumenfeld, "When Politics Becomes Personal," *Washington Post,* June 19, 1996, p. C1.
8. The classic study is Julius Turner, *Party and Constituency: Pressures on Congress,* 1951; revised by Edward V. Schneir, Jr. (Baltimore, Md.: Johns Hopkins Press, 1970). Also see Warren E. Miller and Donald E. Stokes, "Constituency Influence in Congress," 57 *American Political Science Review* (March 1963) and John W. Kingdon, *Congressmen's Voting Decisions* (New York: Harper and Row, 1973). For a finding that the impact of background influences varies according to the broad policy category concerned, see Aage R. Clausen, *How Congressmen Decide: A Policy Focus* (New York: St. Martin's Press, 1973). For the influence of personality upon political decisions, see Fred I. Greenstein, *Personality and Politics* (New York: W.W. Norton and Co., 1975), particularly chapter 3. My categories are comparable to those developed by James David Barber in *The Presidential Character* (Englewood Cliffs, N.J.: Prentice-Hall), 1972. Barber's presidents are more like U.S. senators than are the Connecticut state legislators Barber studied in *The Lawmakers: Recruitment and Adaptation to Legislative Life* (New Haven: Yale University Press, 1965).
9. *The Cambridge Encyclopedia,* 1990, p. 927.
10. For his studies of individual senators, Richard F. Fenno, Jr., utilizes a very simple theoretical framework centered on the interaction between governing, which largely takes place in Washington, and campaigning, which mostly occurs in the home state. See *The Making of a Senator: Dan Quayle* (Washington, D.C.: Congressional Quarterly Press, 1989), pp. viii–ix.

CHAPTER 2

Personality

Becoming the Sons of Their Fathers

Personality is the label applied to an individual's habitual mode of dealing with the world in general and with other persons in particular. The traits making up a personality are numerous and varied. Many are best described as choices or dichotomies. Is one's approach to life optimistic, or is it pessimistic? Are habits of personal hygiene slovenly, or fastidious? Are relationships with others marked by the gregariousness of an outgoing personality, or is the individual shy and inward-looking?

Successful politicians are seldom described as shy. They exhibit strong self-esteem, which supports their apparent belief that their solutions to political problems should be embraced by all. Such self-assurance is not achieved overnight; it is born in childhood and developed over a life span. This confidence, based on the certainty of their own identities, grew in Richard Lugar and Paul Sarbanes from their earliest years, but in contrasting circumstances. Lugar belonged to the fifth generation of his family born in Indiana, while Sarbanes was the first child of his family to be born in America.

The Legacy of a Hoosier Republican

During the Gilded Age, the entrepreneurs of Indianapolis built their factories on railroad spurs or the bank of the White River. A young Indianapolis native, Thomas L. Green, applied the factory principle to baking. Richard Lugar, his grandson, describes Green, who had only five years of formal schooling, as "a classic Horatio Alger case, somebody who started a bicycle shop, which burned down four times, but went on to invent machinery that mass produces cookies and crackers."[1]

In 1896, Green built a brick-walled factory on Miley Avenue in Indianapolis which is still the home of the Thomas L. Green Manufacturing Company. From that factory, baking equipment has gone around the world—equipment which mixes dough, shapes it, places it on moving sheets to pass through ovens up to six hundred feet long, seasons the product, and packages it for sale. Green machinery presently makes products ranging from dog biscuits to frozen pizza.

In 1906, Thomas Green's only child, Bertha, was born. In due course, she attended Butler University of Indianapolis. On a blind date, she met Marvin L. Lugar, a student at Purdue two years her senior. Their courtship was facilitated by their common membership in the Methodist Church.

Marvin Lugar's great-grandfather, George Lugar, immigrated into central Indiana from Germany, by way of Virginia, in 1823. There is a Lugar Creek in Grant County, northeast of Indianapolis, which he named after himself in 1828. George's son, Joseph, fought in the Civil War; his portrait, dressed in his Union officer's uniform, graced Marvin Lugar's home. Dick Lugar's grandfather based his career in animal husbandry, establishing a prosperous livestock commission business in Indianapolis. Upon college graduation, Marvin Lugar entered the business.

In 1930, Marvin Lugar purchased with his father-in-law's help a 611-acre farm, at Depression prices, near the southern boundary of Marion County, on the bank of the White River. The farm raised soybeans, grain, and hogs; it was a natural adjunct to the livestock commission business, which provided a basic service and remained a viable enterprise during the Depression.

Marvin and Bertha's first son, Richard Green Lugar, was born on April 4, 1932. His brother, Tom, was born barely a year later; the two boys grew up together as companions, more like twins than rival siblings. They were taken to the farm in the summer and soon were pulling volunteer corn from the soybean fields for ten cents an hour. Thomas L. Green passed away, leaving the majority interest in his company to Bertha. In 1939, a daughter, Anne, was born. In 1940, the Lugars moved to a colonial-style mansion on elm-lined Washington Boulevard; Dick Lugar said it was "one of the more spectacular residential neighborhoods" of Indianapolis.

Marvin Lugar believed that his financial success was achieved despite the programs of the New Deal. He later returned all the Roosevelt dimes he received in change to symbolize his rejection of FDR and all his works. His political convictions were Republican and conservative, and he felt that his family had no need to hear opposing opinions. He allowed them to listen to only one radio program at dinner time: the conservative commentary of Fulton Lewis, Jr.

In 1940, the Lugars were delighted when a Hoosier champion rose to challenge the hold of Franklin D. Roosevelt on the White House. Richard Lugar's first political memory is of his father by the radio, keeping track with pencil and paper of the roll calls at the 1940 Republican National Convention, as the galleries chanted "We want Willkie!" Dick Lugar says that he has never thought of himself as anything but a Republican.

In 1946, Dick Lugar entered Shortridge, the city's only high school oriented toward college-bound students. The student body of about eighteen hundred students was racially and economically homogeneous. Academic competition was part of the atmosphere of striving at Shortridge; good grades were considered a social asset. Extracurricular activities demonstrated the "well-rounded citizen" that colleges looked for during the era. Already an Eagle Scout, Lugar entered essay contests and oratorical skirmishes, attended Boy's State, and headed the state champion debate team. He played the cello in the school orchestra. He was involved in freshman football, basketball, and track; he was on the varsity track team as a sophomore, but asthma forced him to withdraw when he was a junior. He was founding president of the Key Club and a member of the senior class council. He ran for class president in both his junior and senior years, losing narrowly on both occasions.

Disappointment in politics did not affect Lugar's academic competitiveness. He became valedictorian of the senior class, an accomplishment which he recalled took "a very stiff push." Sarah Singer recalls Dick Lugar in the classroom.

We competed for A plusses those years, in Latin and English classes. He was always raising his hand in class to refute any of my comments, in a classic debater style. It was very annoying for me.

She also criticized the social environment of Shortridge High School.

Unfortunately, college-oriented notions at our high school included ideas about social clubs modeled after Midwest college fraternities and sororities. So our school had some 20 secret clubs: terrible groups with black-balling, pins, and ranking. These clubs organized dances, in season, at local nightclub-halls, every weekend. The girls had a

chance to wear long dresses and receive orchid corsages; fancy bands
played—I remember Louis Armstrong one evening.[2]

Dick Lugar did not join in the social club scene at Shortridge. He felt
the clubs were divisive and destructive of school unity. In his senior year,
Lugar organized a campaign against them. Using the Key Club as a fo-
rum, a meeting of all senior men was held; the issue was debated and a
majority voted against continuation of the social clubs. The Key Club had
no authority to implement the resolution, but its passage served to undermine the clubs' prestige.

This was Lugar's first substantive political success, when the issue,
rather than popularity, carried the day. Significantly, he won the debate in
a public arena he selected, consciously or not, to showcase his own skills.
James David Barber writes that the three roles of a political leader are
rhetoric, personal relations, and homework. A leader will be competent
in all three, but will tend to emphasize one role over the others. Barber
also claims that the best means of predicting a politician's style at the
summit of the profession is to expect the repetition of the first political
success.[3] These findings apply to Dick Lugar. He is not a barn-burning
orator, but he is verbally extremely fluent. He instinctively turns first to
rhetoric as a tool of influence.

Lugar sought a liberal arts college, preferably in the Midwest, but
outside Indiana. He chose Denison University, a Baptist-founded school
in Granville, Ohio. He went from the highly competitive academic atmosphere of Shortridge High School to a college of about the same size;
Denison's student body numbered less than two thousand. Forty years after his own graduation, and a quarter century as a Denison trustee, Lugar
said that Denison has the reputation in the academic world of being a
party school, considered to rank below the Haverfords and Swarthmores.
But it has always had a first-rate faculty; students eager for learning will
not be disappointed.[4]

In retrospect, Dick Lugar felt that Denison was the right choice: "it
was a smaller coeducational college in which I could really try out once
again every single activity."[5] He majored in economics with a minor in
political science, and he still recalls the names of half a dozen faculty
members who made a difference in his intellectual development.

In his freshman year, Lugar followed the campaign of his hero, Robert A. Taft, for reelection as U.S. senator from Ohio. Taft's victory, in spite
of labor's opposition resulting from the Taft-Hartley Act, propelled Taft
into the center of presidential politics. In the late summer of 1952, Lugar

was contacted by the Indiana Republican chairman. When he was a student at Shortridge, Lugar had delivered the winning oration in an "I Speak for Democracy" contest, which the chairman had heard and remembered two years later. He asked Lugar to reestablish the Marion County (Indianapolis) Young Republican Club, which had disintegrated because of divisions between Eisenhower and Taft enthusiasts. Although Lugar favored Taft, he gathered a group of friends—mostly college students who, like himself, were too young to vote. They organized the motorcade for candidate Eisenhower from the airport to Monument Circle in downtown Indianapolis and distributed two tons of confetti to the office workers in buildings around the Circle.

Dick Lugar's first collegiate political achievement came in his junior year, when he won the presidency of the Denison Christian Emphasis Program, which organized a week of study led by visiting theologians. The campaign took him to dormitories and fraternity and sorority houses, where he talked to small groups, claiming that the religion week program should be more vigorous. The electorate consisted of about half the student body.[6] As at Shortridge High, rhetoric brought victory.

The following year, Lugar used this office as the base for a successful campaign in the full student body for co-president of the Denison Campus Government Association. The association elected a man and a woman each year. His counterpart was Charlene Smeltzer, a classmate from Detroit. Dick and Charlene had traded fraternity pins with others. Lugar reports, "At that stage we found each other, and fairly rapidly we were unpinned and then we were pinned again, to each other." But their immediate future called for separation. Charlene was admitted to graduate work in philosophy at Northwestern University, and Dick abandoned vague plans to attend law school when he learned that he would go to Oxford for two years as a Rhodes Scholar, the first ever from Denison University.

When Dick Lugar joined the Rhodes sailing party in September, he met Paul Sarbanes, elected to the Rhodes Scholarship from Maryland. Sarbanes had grown up on Maryland's Eastern Shore, six hundred miles from Indianapolis, in quite a different political culture. The two young men soon discovered common interests: politics and basketball.

The Making of a Maryland Democrat

Spyros Paniotis Sarbanes was born in a tiny mountain village in southern Greece in 1892. Peasant life was hard, and Spyros found an escape in books. But he was unable to pursue formal education beyond the eighth grade, as the village contained no high school. At age sixteen, he immigrated to the United States, joining other members of his extended family. He lived and worked, mainly in Greek restaurants, in New York City, then in Springfield, Massachusetts. Around 1915, he traveled with two cousins along the Atlantic seacoast, seeking business opportunities. They found the town of Salisbury, on Maryland's Eastern Shore, with a candy kitchen for sale on the main street, which they purchased.

Situated at the headwaters of the Wicomico River, Salisbury was established in 1732 as a market center to serve the area's tobacco plantations. By the twentieth century, the town was inbred, suspicious of strangers, Protestant, Democratic, and small—it attained a population of 13,000 by 1940 and grew to 16,429 in 1980. Men of the area were devoted to life on the Chesapeake, to fishing, oystering, and duck hunting. These passions, and the Eastern Shore culture, have been celebrated in James Michener's novel *Chesapeake*. The four young Greeks were an exotic addition to this stable and isolated community. Accepted on their own terms, they made a success of the candy store.

Late in World War I, Spyros Sarbanes enlisted in the United States Navy, proud to serve his adopted land. The navy sent him to sea as a mess steward. After the Armistice took effect, Sarbanes learned that the candy kitchen had burned down, and the navy mustered him out. The partnership was dissolved because the cousins had contracted tuberculosis and were entering a sanitorium. Spyros Sarbanes purchased a two-story building across the street from the candy shop. He opened the Mayflower Grill, recalling in its name the immigrants who landed at Plymouth Rock. Sarbanes embarked on years of unceasing toil, keeping the restaurant open for long hours, then spending more hours with his growing library upstairs. He taught himself to read English and to speak it without an accent.

Established after nine years as a successful businessman, the time came for Spyros Sarbanes to select a wife. Early in 1931, a cousin visited him to tell of the attractions of a young woman named Matina Tsigounis, nineteen years junior to Spyros, who had immigrated the year before and was living with an uncle in Wilmington, Delaware. In October, Spyros embarked on a voyage back to Greece to visit his mother. On the way to New York, he called on the relatives to meet Matina, adopting an assumed name to avoid commitments. No sooner had introductions been accomplished than the cousin who had called on him in Salisbury entered the home, exclaiming, "That's not a Koulouris, that is the Sarbanes from Salisbury!"[7]

Spyros Sarbanes had made his decision. He explained himself to Matina's uncle and proposed that he marry Matina when he returned from Greece. After consulting her brothers, Matina consented. They were married on February 24, 1932.

The bride discovered that there was only one other Greek family in all of Wicomico County. The Misses Leeds and Tilley, who operated a hat shop next to the Mayflower Grill, invited Matina Sarbanes to tea day after day, communicating with smile and gesture, until she began to learn English.

Matina's first child, a son, was born on February 3, 1933. Spyros Sarbanes admonished his children to take pride in their dual heritage: to be proud of being Greek, but prouder still of being American. The duality was symbolized in the name Spyros gave his firstborn. His Greek name would be Paniotis Spyros, reversing Spyros's own names, as they had been reversed by his father; every Greek oldest son is thus named after his grandfather. But Paniotis is translated as Peter. For his son's English name, Spyros Sarbanes chose Paul Spyros Sarbanes.

Paul Sarbanes lived above the Mayflower Grill for the first eight years of his life. His mother devoted full time to his care; they spoke only Greek, as she did not wish him to learn broken English from her. At age four, he was enrolled in Mrs. Harold's Kindergarten School.

The undistracted attention given Paul by his mother is precisely the kind of nurturing that Alfred Adler describes in his study of the influence of birth order on psychological development. Firstborns have measurably higher intelligence, greater social presence when with adults, and greater self-esteem. Firstborn sons are overrepresented among the members of the U.S. Congress and other prestigious occupations. Trauma comes for the firstborn when a sibling is born; this is called the "fear of dethrone-ment."[8] Thus it is important that Paul Sarbanes' brother, Anthony, was not born until Paul was five, and his interests had expanded beyond the home, both socially and linguistically.

Paul Sarbanes remembers the hospitality of the Misses Tilley and Leeds; he spent hours in their hat shop as a toddler. He also remembers riding his tricycle around the main business block of Salisbury at age seven, greeting the shopkeepers he passed. The family's sense of place and belonging was very strong; says Paul, "My memory of Salisbury is of a lot of people taking an interest in us."

This secure beginning provided the foundation for a life of hard work and early responsibility. Sarbanes' labor in the restaurant began when he was tall enough to push a broom, wash glasses, and stand behind the cash register, making the right change. The days were full: school, work in the restaurant, work at home. Grades were expected to be all As; Paul and Anthony, were told that any punishment allotted them at school would be doubled at home. The boys never tested that policy.[9]

Along with his other responsibilities, Sarbanes found time for athletics. When the baseball season was over, he practiced basketball. In 1946, he entered Wicomico County High School, maintained for the white students of Salisbury; blacks attended a school on the other side of town. When Paul went out for the basketball squad, the coach had to persuade Spyros Sarbanes that Paul should be released from work in the restaurant to attend practice. Spyros was an eager convert; he attended every game Paul played in, both at home and away. The basketball squad won its league championship and lost the state championship by a single point. Paul was the star forward.

To sharpen its skills, the team scrimmaged with the team at Maryland State College, an institution for blacks in the nearby town of Princess Anne. As the championship playoffs neared, this team came to watch a regular game in Salisbury. Doorkeepers wanted to deny the blacks admission, but Paul and the Salisbury team threatened to not play, and the visiting team was admitted to sit behind the Salisbury bench and join in the cheering.

A former Salisbury neighbor of the Sarbaneses remembers the intolerant atmosphere of the area. He describes the trip across the Bay Bridge to the Eastern Shore: "You drive ten miles to the East, and that takes you three hundred miles to the South."[10] Attitudes on the isolated Eastern Shore recalled those of the deep South, and many Eastern Shore residents resented the sudden influx of people and automobiles carried by the Chesapeake Bay Bridge, built after World War II. Growing up in racist surroundings, how did Paul Sarbanes avoid absorbing racist values? Sarbanes believes the reason was his father.

> He had a very strong sense of values that he taught us. He was always concerned to treat people decently and fairly. I remember one time I had mistreated the help, or he thought I had. And I really got it, for that. He had a very strong sense of every person's worth and dignity, that they ought to be treated with respect, regardless of whatever their position or station was. And I think we learned that lesson from him.[11]

Paul Sarbanes grew up in the warmth and security of a small town where his father had won a respected place after a decade's residence. The family weathered the Depression without psychic scars because the May-

flower Grill was the only restaurant in downtown Salisbury until long after World War II. Sarbanes suffered no pains of assimilation. He took his
dual Greek and American heritage for granted as a child, appreciated it as
an adult, and used it to raise campaign funds as a politician.

In his final year of high school, Sarbanes narrowly missed election as
president of his class. That same year, a Princeton alumnus called on the
principal to inquire whether there were any Salisbury students that
Princeton should be interested in. Without this inquiry, Sarbanes would
not have considered the Ivy League. He graduated second in his class and
was admitted to Princeton, financing his studies with a combination of jobs
and a scholarship. When he made the varsity basketball squad as a sophomore, his scholarship was increased to permit dropping one of the jobs.

At Princeton, Sarbanes' world expanded enormously. The distance to
Princeton, New Jersey, from Wicomico County, Maryland, is not great; the
expansion of social and intellectual horizons was very great. Studies were
challenging and the faculty distinguished; Paul majored in international affairs, capped by a senior thesis on civil liberties in the United States.

Sarbanes had never known the kind of prep school graduate who set
the social tone of Princeton in the 1950s, but he was as much at ease with
Princeton students as he had been with the Salisbury kindergarteners. As
a sophomore, he was elected by classmates to the Undergraduate Council,
then appointed Council president by his fellow members.

Central to the student social structure were the once exclusive eating
clubs. Students were elected to the clubs at the end of the sophomore
year, and the clubs became the focus of their social life for the final two
college years. Students not elected to one of the clubs could continue to
live in the dormitories but would have to take their meals in town. By the
1950s, the clubs were electing nearly everybody, which redoubled the an-
guish of the few, mostly Jewish, who were excluded. Even after forty years,
Paul Sarbanes' voice hardened as he recalled the injustice.

> It was very brutal for the people who were left out . . . Here these
> people had been admitted to Princeton, were part of the Princeton
> undergraduate body, yet the thing was structured in such a way that
> they could in effect be excluded from an important dimension of
> undergraduate life . . . That's not an acceptable system.[12]

Sarbanes led a challenge to the system, insisting that the clubs accept
the "one hundred percent principle"—that all students would receive at
least one invitation to join an eating club. His role was to

meet with representatives of the club system and heatedly assert that this was an intolerable situation, pressuring the clubs to remedy the situation; and some of them moved in and did so.[13]

This was Sarbanes' first substantive political victory; and his achievement resulted more from private discussion than from public presentation. Recall Barber's classification of essential political roles: personal relations, rhetoric, and homework. Sarbanes depended on personal relations, not rhetoric, although he never slighted his homework. Sarbanes became a politician's politician, able in campaign debate to verbally devastate his opponents, yet preferring to exercise political influence quietly, in private surroundings.

During the 1952 presidential election campaign, a survey showed that two thirds of the Princeton faculty supported the election of Princetonian Adlai Stevenson, but two thirds of the students supported Dwight Eisenhower. Paul organized a Princetonians for Stevenson group that helped with the New Jersey campaign.

In December 1953, he was elected to the Rhodes Scholarship.

Future Senators Growing Up

Entering the world ten months apart, near the midpoint of the generation born between 1925 and 1942, Paul Sarbanes and Dick Lugar shared the experiences of their age cohort within American society. Theirs was labeled the Silent Generation. The Silents were seen as eager to play a role in corporate America, interested in improving the system's procedures, but little interested in rebellion. As Strauss and Howe put it, the Silent Generation was born in a birthrate trough to overly protective parents; its members were docile in school, monogamous in relationships, and conformist upon entering the work force. Overshadowed in youth by the GI generation that won a world war and created a superpower, the other-directed Silents grew to maturity in awe of their juniors, the Boomers (products of the famous baby boom). The Boomers were an inner-directed crowd prone to quick moral judgments, the "me" generation. The Silent Generation provided early leadership for the civil rights and feminist movements, and "Silent professionals account for the 1960s surge in the 'helping professions' (teaching, medicine, ministry, government) and for the 1970s explosion in 'public interest' advocacy groups."[14] Thus Sarbanes and Lugar share the dominant attitudes and personality traits exhibited in the aggregate by their generation. They also share certain traits with each other.

Both Dick Lugar and Paul Sarbanes were firstborn sons. In Sarbanes' case, the special loving attention of his mother continued for five years before his brother Anthony was born. By then, his horizons were expanding, and he mastered English, in a private kindergarten. Dick Lugar's brother Tom followed him so quickly into the family as to be more like a twin than a competing sibling. A daughter was born to the Lugars when Dick was seven and to the Sarbaneses when Paul was nine. As firstborns, both Sarbanes and Lugar developed a firm sense of identity, demonstrated an early aptitude for learning, and were sensitive to adult standards. Because they experience support and reward from their environment, firstborns develop self-confidence and social skills that carry them to adult positions of leadership. In this basic sense, the personalities of Lugar and Sarbanes were, and are, similar. From their earliest days, both future senators exhibited a natural gregariousness based on a secure sense of self-worth. Each feels at home in the midst of a crowd.

Both families were nurturing, and both sets of parents were strong willed and established firm standards. The Sarbaneses' circumstances were modest. Paul Sarbanes' work in the restaurant was genuinely needed to bolster the family fortunes. Paul says the lack of idle hours was never a hardship. Anthony Sarbanes adds that their home "was not run as a democracy. The work ethic was very strong."

The elder Lugars were equally dedicated to the work ethic, and they could point to their own improving circumstances as its reward. Their sons worked on the farm at a tender age, but this was more an object lesson than an economic necessity. One year, Marvin Lugar encouraged each of them to invest seventeen dollars they had earned a dime at a time weeding soybeans in an acre of wheat. They expected to double their money with the harvest. But the White River flooded, wiping out both acres. Their father did not return their investment; he wanted them to learn the reality of risk. The boys later purchased a sow, which returned substantial profit through many litters.

Their fathers were strong presences in both families, providing firm role models for their sons. Paul Sarbanes followed his father's example by becoming a reader; this led to a joint appreciation of intellectual matters which culminated in Spyros Sarbanes engaging his son's Princeton teachers in intense conversations. Both fathers expressed strong political values; and here the divergence was marked. Spyros Sarbanes was devoted to Franklin D. Roosevelt; Paul says simply, "There was a lot of respect for

Roosevelt in the household." Marvin Lugar despised the New Deal and all its works; he saw no need for his family even to hear the Democratic side of the political discussion. And the Civil War, which made northern Indiana Republican, was ever present in the portrait of Great-grandfather Lugar as a Union officer.

Both Sarbanes and Lugar narrowly missed election as class president in their high school senior years. Their academic achievements probably made them too popular with their teachers to win popularity contests among their peers. Both won elections in college. This achievement by Paul Sarbanes was particularly striking, because he came to Princeton as an outsider.

Both future senators challenged school social arrangements in the name of wider participation, Lugar attacking the social clubs of Shortridge High School, and Sarbanes challenging the exclusive Princeton eating clubs. These were their first substantive political victories. Their different actions in these contests suggested divergent future political styles. Lugar followed the rhetorical route, basing his political efforts on public speech. Sarbanes was successful in private negotiations. The basic difference in their modes of relating as senators to their constituents is that Dick Lugar talks to people; his rostrum can easily become a pulpit. Paul Sarbanes listens to people, standing in the midst of the crowd.

The lasting impact of their childhood and youth was the development of their personalities. Gregarious, taking a genuine interest in the welfare of others, they easily rose to the kind of leadership that, in a democracy, becomes a basis for political power. The differences between their political attitudes and partisanship were clearly related to the contrasting political values of their parents, particularly their fathers, and the differing circumstances of their families. These values, and the partisan attachments they implied, were formed in the aftermath of the Depression and refined by later experience.

Notes

1. Interview with Senator Lugar, September 1977.
2. Letter to the author from Sarah Eleanor Singer, April 11, 1983.
3. James David Barber, *The Presidential Character* (Englewood Cliffs, N.J.: Prentice-Hall, 1972), pp. 7–10, 99.
4. Interview with Senator Lugar, July 19, 1991.
5. Interview, December 21, 1982.
6. Interview, December 16, 1996.

7. Interview with Mrs. Matina Sarbanes, September 1982.
8. See Raymond J. Corsini, ed., *Encyclopedia of Psychology* (New York: John Wiley & Sons, 1984), vol. 1, pp. 15–17, 152–156.
9. This account of his youth is based on interviews with Senator Sarbanes in 1982 and 1991 and interviews with Matina Sarbanes and Anthony Sarbanes in September 1982. Also see the profile of Sarbanes written by Doug Birch, the *Baltimore Sun* January 31, February 1 and 2, 1988.
10. Interview with Charles Cochran, May 28, 1991.
11. Interview with Senator Sarbanes, July 5, 1982.
12. Interview, December 12, 1991.
13. Interview, December 16, 1996.
14. William Strauss and Neil Howe, *Generations: The History of America's Future, 1584–2069* (New York: William Morrow, 1991), pp. 179–288; quotation from p. 285.

CHAPTER 3

Ideology and
the Growth of Ambition

Cecil John Rhodes went to Africa at age seventeen to seek his fortune, then returned to England periodically over eight years to fulfill the three-year residence requirement for obtaining a degree from Oxford. Rhodes achieved his fortune by amalgamating the major diamond mining enterprises, then rose in colonial politics to become twice prime minister of the Cape Colony. When he died in 1902, his will established a scheme of scholarships for young men at Oxford, each selected for attributes "likely to guide him to esteem the performance of public duties as his highest aim," from the British Empire, the United States, and Germany. By bringing future leaders of these nations to share a common education and common friends, Rhodes hoped to further the twin causes of world peace and material progress.[1]

Since 1903, when the first Scholars were admitted, the Rhodes benefaction has made a measurable impact on the ancient university, which produced many officials of British imperialism but had not yet become truly international in its interests or student body. The Rhodes bequest's importance was recognized as early as 1911, when the Oxford Secretary of the Rhodes Trust was awarded an honorary degree. Rhodes Scholars found a literary niche that same year with the publication of Max Beerbohm's satirical novel, *Zuleika Dobson*.

Beerbohm had his main undergraduate character, the Duke of Dorset, conclude that the American Rhodes Scholars, with their eagerness to please and their delight in those aspects of Oxford that English undergraduates took for granted, were a "noble" influence on the social life of

the University. Then Beerbohm introduced Abimilech V. Oover, the pro-
totypical American Rhodes Scholar. A practiced orator, Oover was given
to making public speeches to private gatherings; he would orate in ful-
some phrases to an audience of two or three. He articulated high moral
sentiments and was able to join reverently in a toast to Church and State,
"despite his passionate mental reservation in favor of Pittsburgh-
Anabaptism and the Republican Ideal."[2]

In 1988 I happened to discuss *Zuleika Dobson* with the late Sir Edgar
Williams, who was Oxford Secretary of the Rhodes Trust and Warden of
Rhodes House from 1952 to 1980. He remarked that Rhodes Scholars are
no longer like Oover. "The one who came closest to it in my time," he
added, "was Dick Lugar." The comparison was striking. Dick Lugar entered the student political life of Denison University as the president of
the Christian Endeavor Program. In his sixties as in his twenties, Lugar's
speech in casual conversation consists of complete paragraphs delivered
in the measured cadences one would expect from a Methodist lay minister, which he is. Lugar's conversational style was established before he
went to Oxford, but he found many occasions to practice it there.

Rhodes Scholars do not arrive in Oxford as blank slates; they are sent
there because of potential displayed and attitudes already formed. They
enter Oxford on the cusp of maturity, with established political ideologies, the interconnected ideas that govern the individual's understanding
of the political world. What is not so well settled—despite whatever
grand visions were told to Rhodes selection committees—is the direction
that will be given to the scholar's life by those ideas. Where will ambition
lead?

A Balliol Scholar

When Paul Sarbanes, a second-generation Greek-American, won a
Rhodes Scholarship, his victory was celebrated as a realization of the
American dream. The Voice of America sent a camera crew to Salisbury
to show his family and the Mayflower Grill, then to Princeton to record
Sarbanes among his classmates and at the helm of student government.
The film had no sound track; that was added when the film was distributed in Greece. Spyros Sarbanes obtained a copy of the film, which was
discovered years later in the Salisbury house, and has supplied images for
his senator son's campaign commercials.

Advised by Princeton Oxonians, Sarbanes applied for admission to Balliol College. He felt that Balliol sounded like "an interesting and congenial place, more open and egalitarian than some of the other large colleges." Founded in 1260, Balliol has been regarded since the mid-nineteenth century as one of the most intellectually distinguished of Oxford's thirty-five colleges. The colleges are separate communities in which a few hundred undergraduates come together with a few dozen faculty members.

Sarbanes sampled the varied activities that Oxford offered. He was active in the junior common room (the undergraduate social organization) and rowed in one of the college eights, which trained through the spring term until the Eights Week races in June. And he joined the university basketball squad. Sarbanes played guard in the game against Cambridge; Dick Lugar was the other guard; and Oxford won. Playing against Cambridge qualified them for a "half blue," the equivalent of a letter; "half" because basketball was considered a minor sport.

Sarbanes' gregariousness had an impact. Without seeking the position, he was elected vice president of the Balliol junior common room for his second year.[3] Thus Sarbanes followed Oover, Beerbohm's model Rhodes Scholar, by taking delight in something the British students took for granted: with examinations comfortably far off, there was ample time for activities outside the curriculum. But Paul heard the call to intellectual endeavor very plainly. He began in the popular undergraduate program in Philosophy, Politics, and Economics (PPE), established at Oxford after World War I in response to pressures to offer studies in economics. Before his studies were well launched, Sarbanes was recruited into a new graduate program. But Oxford's undergraduate colleges in the 1950s made few provisions for graduate students, who were thought capable of conducting independent research with little guidance. After several months, Sarbanes realized that graduate students were on the periphery of college life. Unwittingly, he had placed himself in a position like that of the Princeton students who failed to be elected by an eating club. Sarbanes was granted a third scholarship year to complete the PPE program.

Early in the summer after his first year, Paul Sarbanes organized an Oxford University basketball trip to Romania under mildly false pretenses; the Romanians may have expected a team of Englishmen, for whom basketball is a minor sport; they were confronted by Americans, with one Canadian. Sarbanes invited Dick Lugar to join this expedition, but Lugar declined, as Charlene Smeltzer was coming to visit him during that vacation.

When the basketball tour finished, Sarbanes met his mother in

Greece. It was Matina Sarbanes' first return to her native land since emigrating to the United States. Sarbanes visited the temples of ancient Greek democracy and the haunts of the Athenian philosophers. He also came to understand his parents' roots in the dusty mountain villages of their birth.

Returning to Oxford, Sarbanes focused on the PPE syllabus, writing essays for tutors in two different subjects each week, spending mornings to research the essays. Far more than at Princeton, Sarbanes found himself among politically congenial friends. Only two or three of the thirty-two American Rhodes Scholars could be identified as Republicans; most shared Sarbanes' enthusiasm for Adlai Stevenson. In fact, the Silent Generation supported Stevenson more earnestly than did any other American age group.[4]

Sarbanes had time to think of the future. Paul Sheats, later a professor of English at UCLA, was also elected to the Rhodes Scholarship from Maryland in 1954. Sheats remembers Sarbanes in the Balliol College garden, musing about the attractions of a seat in the U.S. Senate. Sarbanes remembers a strong interest in public life at the time, but he does not recall thinking of particular offices.[5]

The single event at Oxford which proved most important for Sarbanes' future occurred in the fall of 1956. It happened at a meeting of the Oxford American Association, of which Sarbanes was president, succeeding Dick Lugar. Because of her interest in visiting America, Christine Dunbar attended an association meeting with an American friend. To her astonishment, the young man in charge of the meeting came marching toward her. Says Paul, "I saw this gorgeous English girl, or I guessed English, and I said, 'Gee, I wonder who that is,' so off I went to find out."

Christine picks up the story. "I had never met an American man in my life. There, suddenly, bearing down the length of the hall, is my [future] husband, sticking out his hand and saying, 'What part of the States do you come from?' I sort of gulped and said, 'Well, Brighton, actually.'"

Like Paul Sarbanes, Christine Dunbar was the first member of her family to attend college. A student at St. Hugh's, a women's college founded in 1886, she was studying classical languages; with tongue in cheek, Sarbanes expressed surprise that anyone would study Greek who had no connection with Greece. Christine supported a movement that sought the admission of women as members of the Oxford Union, the debating society that has nurtured many future members of Parliament. Sarbanes kept calling her to inquire about the progress of her cause; Christine realized that he was less interested in the cause than in its proponent.

In May 1957, during Sarbanes' intense preparation for his PPE examinations, he received word of his father's sudden death from a heart attack and stroke. Sarbanes flew home for the funeral but returned to Oxford for the June examinations. Knowing how Spyros Sarbanes prized intellectual accomplishment, Sarbanes may have, in a psychological sense, dedicated his examination efforts to his father's memory. He won the rare accolade of First Class Honours in Philosophy, Politics, and Economics, and he shared Balliol College's Jenkyns Prize in the subject. His promise of intellectual distinction had been fully realized. That fall, he enrolled in Harvard Law School.

The American at Pembroke

Dick Lugar was one of the two winners of the Indiana Rhodes Scholar competition who were sent on to the district selection committee, meeting in Chicago in December 1953. The interviewers knew of Lugar's Young Republican activities in 1952 and had a very negative image of U.S. senator William Jenner, a leading isolationist, and the Indiana Republican party, which Jenner then controlled. The interviewers asked how a single individual could have an impact on such an organization. Lugar recalled in 1982 that

> the selectors asked me whether I would be willing in the future to run for political office, or whether I had the stomach for that and was willing to mix it up and so forth, and I indicated that I did and I would . . . I felt an obligation from that time forward not to let them down.[6]

Appointed to the Scholarship, and committed, like Sarbanes, to the PPE curriculum, Lugar was required to name the Oxford colleges he would like to enter. Researching that question, Lugar came across the name of Pembroke College, described as "small but good," and he was attracted by learning that there were few Americans at Pembroke.

Pembroke more than satisfied Dick Lugar's desire for an atmosphere unaffected by Americans. He was the only resident American. Lugar says he was "a unique specimen," and thus an object of curiosity. In that era, the Pembroke student body was divided between the "hearties," the graduates of certain English public—that is, private—schools, who often acted as the spoiled members of a privileged class, and the students who had obtained their secondary educations at the taxpayers' expense. Lugar was approached by members of the latter faction, who asked him to be a candidate for president of the Pembroke junior common room. Responding to this "genuine draft," Lugar came in second in a three-man race. In the runoff, he was elected.[7] This unusual accomplishment for an American led to Lugar's being designated as the president of the Oxford University American Association for his second year.

Lugar's greatest athletic satisfaction came in playing basketball against Cambridge in the fall of 1954 and thus winning the "half blue." His asthma had prevented his winning a basketball letter in high school or college, but he shared the Hoosier passion for the sport and had practiced it since childhood.

Academically, Oxford represented a more dramatic change from Denison University than the change from Shortridge High School to Denison. "Oxford," he said, "was a more cerebral affair."

> My life I think at that point had been a much more highly disciplined one. Both Shortridge and Denison were highly competitive academic experiences in which I was bound up with quizzes and tests and term papers and the rigors of debate competition or internal political competition. But in Oxford for the first time I really had an opportunity to have lots of time for really extensive projects and reading.[8]

One of the books he read was Russell Kirk's *The Conservative Mind.* Lugar says, "That was my first insight into the scope of Edmund Burke's work . . . That probably is a reasonably good benchmark for much of my philosophical construct." He began to build philosophical support for the conservatism he had already adopted. Lugar would adopt Burke's concern for protecting the relationships of an organic society to justify some of his actions in the Senate.

Lugar also read Joseph Shumpeter's *Capitalism, Socialism, and Democracy.* Burke and Shumpeter wrote on topics he was officially studying, but Lugar also read *The Brothers Karamazov* and, most daunting for sheer length, *War and Peace.* Neither Dostoyevsky nor Tolstoy was part of the PPE requirement. "It was," Lugar says,

> a period in my life in which I really had an opportunity to read extensively all sorts of books, authors, and traditions for the first time and to see a great number of people who were involved in both English and world politics at that time, or in the arts and letters, first hand.

An example was C.S. Lewis, the historian and Christian apologist. Lugar discovered Lewis's *Surprised by Joy,* learned that he was an Oxford don, and went to hear some of his lectures in medieval history.

Although the Rhodes Trustees are pleased to grant a third year as a Rhodes Scholar for almost any academic reason, in the 1950s a Scholar was required to resign the scholarship if he married. In the summer of 1955 Charlene Smeltzer came to England. She and Lugar passed an idyllic few months together, became engaged, and established the wedding date for the fall of 1956. Lugar did not apply for a third Rhodes Scholar year but completed the battery of PPE examinations (the Final Honours School) in June 1956. Tolstoy and C.S. Lewis did not sustain him, but his performance was adequate to win an ordinary B.A. degree. Following the English custom, he would receive an M.A. after five years, upon payment of a fee.

The Korean War ended in 1953. Many of Dick Lugar's generation had been involved in it, and he felt that he owed an obligation to his country. Happily, fulfilling such an obligation was not incompatible with marriage. Near the end of his final year at Pembroke, Lugar visited the American embassy in London to arrange enlistment in the U.S. Navy.

Ideology and Ambition at Oxford

What was the impact of Oxford on Paul Sarbanes and Dick Lugar? Both read PPE, although Sarbanes made an abortive foray into a graduate program. Sarbanes' academic accomplishment was more distinguished than Lugar's; indeed, it was more distinguished than that of about 90 percent of Oxford graduates, as only a handful are awarded first class honors. Both played basketball for the university, and Sarbanes succeeded Lugar as president of the Oxford American Association. Lugar's achievement of this position is particularly striking, because he was a partisan Republican in a group that was overwhelmingly Democratic.

The intellectual impact of Oxford came from more than the PPE curriculum. In Dick Lugar's case, confronting the liberally oriented academic environment made him more sophisticated in defending his conservative beliefs; and this sophistication grew with his study of such works as Kirk's *The Conservative Mind,* even as extracurricular reading reinforced his religious faith. For Paul Sarbanes, an intense study of the PPE syllabus gave him chapter and verse to cite in support of liberal Democratic policies. Oxford did not implant new ideologies. But one result of experiencing other nations and cultures is obvious: both Sarbanes and Lugar ever afterward took a generally internationalist approach to politics. In fact, all seven of the former Rhodes Scholars elected to the Senate have shown an internationalist persuasion.[9] Dick Lugar did not have to repudiate Senator Jenner upon his entry into Indiana politics. The voters had already accomplished that.

Lugar and Sarbanes were in Oxford at a potentially crucial stage in the life cycle, when a young man abandons adolescence to develop a self-image in the adult world. From this psychological viewpoint, we can assert that their time at Oxford fulfilled a function, particularly for Dick Lugar, similar to the role played by Oxford in the development of Cecil Rhodes himself.

Daniel Levinson and his associates defined the adult male life cycle on the basis of periodic interviews with forty American men born between 1923 and 1934. They found a primary ingredient of the transition into early adulthood to be the formulation of "the Dream," a conception, which may be vague or quite specific, of the direction the individual will take in the adult world.[10]

Adopting Levinson's concept, Cecil Rhodes' most recent biographer tells us that Rhodes' Dream was quite specific, if somewhat juvenile. In Oxford in 1877, he wrote a lengthy "Confession of Faith," which set forth the notion of founding a secret society, modeled on the Jesuits, dedicated to expanding the British Empire and reuniting the English-speaking peoples. The final paragraph left Rhodes' fortune to the accomplishment of this end; thus Rhodes first formulated the concept that would evolve into his scholarships. That term at Oxford supplied the twenty-two-year-old Rhodes with a moratorium from the daily entrepreneurial concerns of South Africa to define an adult role for himself. Although vaguely preparing for the law, Rhodes spent most of his Oxford time in conversations and athletic contests with friends of the landed gentry. He neither sought nor attained intellectual distinction.[11] And his intent in establishing the scholarships was not primarily intellectual. Rhodes would be quite comfortable knowing that the first of his Scholars to attain the White House formed intense friendships in two years at Oxford but, like Rhodes himself, never earned a degree.

Dick Lugar's description of relaxing into serious reading projects which were not part of the PPE program suggests a moratorium, rather more intellectual than Rhodes', from the intensely competitive academic environments he had known. Lugar's Dream (in the sense defined by Levinson) had been given a mighty reinforcement by his Rhodes selection interview. The moratorium supplied at Oxford allowed him to further define the Dream, and to test it against reality. He also validated his Dream through success in the only political contests open to him: he became president, first of the Pembroke junior common room, then of the Oxford American Association.

Paul Sarbanes was pointed toward academic accomplishment of a conventional kind; he achieved it magnificently. But these self-generated pressures did not prevent him from perfecting his Dream, as suggested by the scene of Sarbanes contemplating the attractions of public life in the Balliol garden. The Dream was validated by his election as vice president of the Balliol senior common room in his second year and as president of the Oxford American Association for his third year. Both Sarbanes and Lugar could well have launched political careers if they had never attended Oxford. But their years at Oxford helped to solidify their ambitions and provided experiences indicating that those ambitions would be attainable. The ambition to achieve high elective office may have been born already, but at Oxford it took on substance and plausibility.

The romantic futures of both Sarbanes and Lugar were settled at Oxford, Lugar's by his engagement to Charlene Smeltzer, Sarbanes' by the discovery of Christine Dunbar. According to Levinson, an important part of the transition to early adulthood can be the finding of "a special woman" who complements the man's efforts to define his Dream and test it against reality.[12] Thus Lugar and Sarbanes achieved two of the milestones Levinson specifies as central in the transition to adulthood. A third milestone, establishing a mentorship relation, would occur upon their return to the United States.

A Front Row Seat at the Pentagon

Dick Lugar received orders to report to the Navy Officer Candidate School in January 1957. He returned to the United States in the late summer of 1956 to find that his father, chronically ill for several years, could not attend his marriage to Charlene Smeltzer in Detroit.

The young Lugars returned from their honeymoon to find Marvin Lugar very ill; he died in November. Happily for their mother, Lugar's brother Tom returned to Indianapolis from army service a few weeks after Dick and Charlene left in January for the navy.

After Officer Candidate School in Newport, Rhode Island, and Intelligence School in Jacksonville, Florida, Lugar was assigned to the Pentagon, where he became an intelligence briefer for the chief of Naval Operations, the late Admiral Arleigh Burke. It was a heady experience for a junior officer; his contemporaries at Newport referred to "the CNO" in reverential terms normally reserved for the deity.

The Cold War entered one of its warm phases in 1958. The pro-Soviet overtones of a coup in Iraq gave President Eisenhower reason to implement the Eisenhower Doctrine, which promised help to any nation threatened by Communism. In July, President Camille Chamoun of Lebanon asked for a show of force by the United States to bolster his regime against Syrian-based Moslems. Admiral Burke dispatched the Sixth Fleet, which landed five thousand marines in Beirut. Happily, the troops were welcomed by beach-goers in bathing suits, and there was no fighting. Dick Lugar's role in the crisis was to keep the names, positions, and commitments of the various Lebanese officials straight for Admiral Burke.

Several ships steamed from Lebanon through the Suez Canal in August. They traversed the Indian Ocean and entered the South China Sea, where Chinese Communists were shelling the Nationalist Chinese islands of Quemoy and Matsu. Admiral Burke interposed the Seventh Fleet, thus reinforced, into the Taiwan Straits, and the crisis passed by the end of October.[13]

Dick Lugar may have recalled these experiences of the successful threat of force thirty-two years later, when he supported President Bush's preparations for war against Iraq. But the lasting influence came from his relationship with Admiral Burke. When asked what the strongest lesson or impact of the navy experience was, Lugar replied,

> The strongest impact was that Admiral Burke served as a mentor for me in many respects. He was . . . exercising great power and authority. The orders that he issued after seeing the facts involved thousands of people and the expenditure of sometimes tens of millions of dollars, if he would wave a whole fleet backward or forward somewhere, or go into a rather daring maneuver. I had the opportunity to be sort of at his right side as he called the shots, and I think this was very important, just to vicariously think through things as he saw them and to at least watch somebody who had an extraordinarily good batting average in terms of results, as to how he organized great forces, how he delegated responsibility, how he used staff and information, how he worked with people . . . who had information that he wanted.[14]

One of Lugar's duties was to give intelligence briefings by closed circuit television to President Eisenhower from a basement room of the White House. His life off duty contrasted sharply with the sense of involvement in great affairs. The pay of a lieutenant, junior grade, was modest in comparison to the cost of living in the national capital. The Lugars lived in a Washington apartment which was not air conditioned— "As I live through these summers now," Lugar says, "I cannot imagine exactly how that worked"—and Mark, the first of their four sons, was born.

When Lugar's active duty obligation neared its end, associates asked him to remain in the navy, but the family businesses were in increasingly poor condition, and brother Tom wanted help. The Lugars returned to Indianapolis in May 1960 and found a home on the west side of the city. Dick Lugar was named secretary and treasurer of both the Thomas L. Green Manufacturing Co. and the Lugar Stock Farms.

The farm was burdened by a $50,000 loan Marvin Lugar had taken out for business and medical reasons, and the baking machinery plant suffered from obsolescence. The Lugar brothers made an effective team. Tom was an engineering graduate of Purdue and exhibited his Grandfather Green's mechanical ingenuity. Tom solved the engineering problems, while Lugar dealt with finance and legal requirements. In 1962, the brothers borrowed money to buy out the minor stockholders of the Green Company, who were all distant relatives. Dick Lugar's personal investment was $62,000; the brothers each attained a 17 percent share in the Green company. With their mother's 51 percent, the immediate family was firmly in control. They added significant space and capacity to the original factory and aggressively extended its operations.

Four Mentors and Three Levels of Government

In the fall of 1957, Paul Sarbanes entered Harvard Law School. The change from the gentle pace of Oxford bothered him. The Harvard Law curriculum and teaching method were designed to absorb the last ounce of a student's energy and attention.

Sarbanes' interest in politics received practical reinforcement. In 1958, he joined a handful of friends in campaigning for a classmate, Greek-American Michael Dukakis. Dukakis sought one of four seats on the Redevelopment Authority of Brookline, a Boston suburb. Republican Yankees had dominated Brookline politics; Dukakis's grass-roots campaign aimed to replace the Irish, patronage-oriented Democratic organization as the local opposition, in the name of good government.[15]

In June 1960, Sarbanes received his degree cum laude from Harvard Law School. He and Christine Dunbar were married in Christ Episcopal Church of Cambridge, Massachusetts; the groom then went down to Baltimore and passed the Maryland bar examination.

The newlyweds settled in a row house in the Bolton Hill area of downtown Baltimore, an old neighborhood rediscovered by young professional couples, the process that would later be called gentrification. Bolton Hill was across the city from the Greek neighborhood, but Sarbanes joined the Greek Orthodox congregation, a sure point of entry into the Greek community. Christine enrolled at the Episcopal Cathedral and won a faculty appointment to selective Goucher College, then a women's school. A few years later, in an economy move, Goucher closed its classics major program. Christine then became a Latin teacher at the Daniel Coit Gilman School, Baltimore's leading private preparatory school. The Sarbanes children attended a "magnet" public elementary school, then went on to Gilman. Christine noted ruefully that Gilman did not offer a tuition discount to faculty children.

On the recommendation of the Baltimore law firm he had worked in during the summer of 1958, Sarbanes was appointed in the fall of 1960 as the law clerk to Judge Morris Soper of the federal Fourth Circuit Court of Appeals. Having entered politics as a Bull Moose Republican, Judge Soper was then eighty-five and had been on the bench for forty years. He was regarded as one of the most able appeals court judges in the country. Thus Sarbanes' first experience after law school was in the heart of the federal judiciary.

When Judge Soper took his vacation in Florida, Sarbanes was assigned to the Maryland legislature as a bill drafter. He had a chance to assess the quality of the state legislature, and he probably concluded that he could make a difference in that environment. When his clerkship expired, Sarbanes became an associate in the law firm of Piper and Marbury, one of the cornerstones of the Baltimore legal establishment. Partner William L. Marbury's ancestor had been the petitioner in the most famous case in American constitutional history, *Marbury v. Madison*.[16]

After practicing under Marbury's direction for little more than a year, Sarbanes learned from friends of the open position of administrative assistant to Walter Heller, chairman of President Kennedy's Council of Economic Advisers. Sarbanes had a chance to serve his country in a position that could use his Oxford economics training.

The prestige of economics as a discipline was at an apex; Heller talked optimistically of "fine tuning" the engine of American prosperity. "Heller and his associates became the most highly influential and frequently consulted Council of Economic Advisers in history."[17] When Paul Sarbanes joined Heller in 1962, that influence was about to reach its peak. Legislation was being formulated to bring about the historic tax cut of 1963.

The tax structure had been established during World War II to support the war effort and take money from private hands to curb inflation. Heller believed that money taken by the government prevented the private investment that could bring economic growth and full employment. Kennedy rejected Heller's recommendation for a temporary, "quickie" tax cut in 1962, but he supported the concept of tax reform which would make the system more fair. He soon accepted the concept that reform should be accompanied by permanent tax reductions for corporations, to stimulate investment, and for the individuals, some below the official poverty line, most burdened by taxes.

Paul Sarbanes worked at the center of negotiations over the tax bill. Tax reform was soon stalled in Congress, because "[e]very legislator's favorite reform closed some other legislator's favorite loophole."[18] But the tax reduction, eventually signed into law by Lyndon Johnson, prevented an incipient recession and was followed by several years of economic expansion which produced greater tax revenues for the government despite lower rates for corporations and individuals.

Paul Sarbanes' experience with the 1963 tax cut helped him decide, nearly twenty years later, to vote for President Ronald Reagan's somewhat similar tax cut. The greatest lesson of his work in the Executive Office Building next to the White House was to see how Walter Heller operated to convert convictions into policy.

The pace of Washington politics was frantic, and the hours were long. The daily commute on overcrowded highways became an intolerable burden. Sarbanes decided that he would either have to move his family to Washington or give up his position. At that point, he received an offer from a distinguished Baltimore attorney, Frank Murnahan, that he could not refuse. Murnahan was slated to chair a commission of notable citizens charged with modernizing Baltimore's city charter. He asked Paul to serve as executive director of the commission's staff.

The dramatic solution of metropolitan area government, which excited Indianapolis in the same era, was not available. Baltimore City is, in the state system, the equivalent of one of Maryland's twenty-three counties; it is entirely independent of neighboring Baltimore County. Baltimore then elected independently both a mayor and a controller; the controller headed an independent financial operation; in well-run cities, these functions are performed by a line department under the mayor. The revised charter established a new Department of Finance and assigned the function of auditor to the former controller. Other changes were made in the appointive powers of the mayor and in the functions of the hospital commission. Sarbanes was proud of accomplishing the charter changes in a single year; the recommendations were passed by the commission, adopted by the city council, and approved by the voters in a referendum.

In 1965, on the invitation of Frank Murnahan, a senior partner, Sarbanes became associated with the law firm of Venable, Baetjer, and Howard. Sarbanes practiced corporate law, primarily under the direction of Frank Murnahan. The role of mentor, which Admiral Burke served for Dick Lugar, was performed for Sarbanes by a succession of four distinguished men who provided examples of the judicial temperament and the careful weighing of policy choices.

> I had a string of [such influences]. I had Judge Soper, then Mr. Marbury, the senior partner of the law firm, then Walter Heller. Then I came back to work for Frank Murnahan. Thus I had, in succession, four really able people for whom I worked. Mr. Soper was considered one of the best Court of Appeals judges; Mr. Marbury was regarded as the best lawyer in Maryland; and Heller, who I think is an outstanding economist; and then Frank Murnahan, who is now a Fourth Circuit Court of Appeals judge.[19]

What common thread ran through this association with two lawyers, a judge, and an economist? Sarbanes says it was their example of making decisions that would last.

The Return of the Natives

Paul Sarbanes and Dick Lugar returned from Oxford a year apart. Both made the key decision that would lead them into elective politics: they returned to their native states.

Dick Lugar entered the navy. Stationed at the Pentagon, he saw international relations in their ultimate aspect of naked power. Sarbanes continued his formal education for three years at Harvard Law School. Then he worked in the Kennedy administration. Both Sarbanes and Lugar had an early taste of the life of the national capital and of politics as practiced by experts.

This period of their lives reinforced their political ideologies, just as the Oxford experience had strengthened them. After serving under a leading Cold Warrior, Lugar became a successful small businessman, demonstrating to himself the virtues of hard work and risk-taking in the free enterprise system. Paul Sarbanes had barely embarked upon the practice of law when he became a staff member, first for a federal judge, then for the Maryland legislature, next for a leading member of the Kennedy administration, and finally for a Baltimore governmental commission. If it is the hallmark of liberal attitudes to believe that government can make a beneficial difference, Sarbanes experienced that difference in local, state, and national politics; and he found that he could make a difference in government.

In another of the striking parallels in their life stories, their fathers died within half a year of each other. This bereavement may have made both men more receptive to the mentorship relations they developed soon afterward. According to Daniel Levinson, the mentor is a transitional figure who may serve as teacher, sponsor, host, or guide to the world a young man is entering. Most importantly, the mentor supports and facilitates the realization of the Dream, "helping to define the newly emerging self in its newly discovered world."[20]

Sarbanes and Lugar encountered, on their return from Oxford, distinguished men who served as role models of the successful political practitioner. Dick Lugar volunteered the term "mentor" in describing Admiral Arleigh Burke; Paul Sarbanes tends to use "influences" to describe the four able men he worked under after graduating from law school.

Ideology guides political choices; it can also decide life choices. Lugar and Sarbanes went to Oxford as young adults, with ideologies well formed. At Oxford, where both enjoyed a kind of moratorium after hectic undergraduate lives, the interconnected concepts of ideology coalesced into a more specific ambition, pointing toward elective office. And their achievements in Oxford made political careers seem attainable. Then, when they returned to their native states, both served with mentors who personified successful political achievement. They began to live with political ambition as a constant companion.

42 REASONABLE DISAGREEMENT

Notes

1. Robert I. Rotberg, *The Founder: Cecil Rhodes and the Pursuit of Power* (New York: Oxford University Press, 1988).

2. Max Beerbohm, *Zuleika Dobson* (London: Penguin Books, 1952), p. 95. (First published, 1911.)

3. Interview with Frank Sieverts, June 13, 1993. Sieverts entered Balliol as a Rhodes Scholar in the fall of 1955. After a distinguished career as a foreign service officer, he became a staff member of the Senate Foreign Relations Committee, where he worked with both Lugar and Sarbanes.

4. Strauss and Howe, *Generations*, p. 285.

5. This account of Paul Sarbanes' time at Oxford depends upon interviews with Senator Sarbanes, Mrs. Matina Sarbanes, Mrs. Christine Dunbar Sarbanes, and Paul Sheats.

6. Interview with Senator Lugar, December 21, 1982. Senator Lugar confirmed in 1991 that he felt that his Rhodes selection was "a vote for advocacy within this Republican party milieu." But he had no idea at the time just how the obligation might come to be fulfilled. Interview of July 19, 1991.

7. Interview, December 16, 1996.

8. Interview, December 21, 1982. This account of Lugar's Oxford days is also drawn from the interviews of March 18, 1983, July 19, 1991, and December 16, 1996.

9. Five former Rhodes Scholars (Fulbright, Lugar, Sarbanes, Pressler, and Feingold) have taken seats on the Foreign Relations Committee, and two (Fulbright and Lugar) have chaired it. David Boren of Oklahoma pursued an interest in international relations as member and then chair of the Select Committee on Intelligence. Bill Bradley of New Jersey was a member of the Intelligence Committee and chair of the Subcommittee on International Debt of the Finance Committee.

10. Daniel J. Levinson, *The Seasons of a Man's Life* (New York: Knopf, 1978), pp. 91–93. Levinson uses the initial capital to emphasize the significance of "the Dream."

11. Rotberg, *The Founder*, pp. 96–102. It is doubtful that Levinson's *Seasons* is totally applicable to nineteenth-century Victorian Englishmen, but Rotberg makes an excellent case for the use of this particular concept.

12. Levinson, *Seasons*, pp. 109–110. Remember that Levinson wrote about the Silent generation. Persons born after 1942 may be appalled at the sexist notion of "a special woman."

13. For a brief account of naval operations during the period, see Kenneth J. Hagan, *This People's Navy: The Making of American Sea Power* (New York: Free Press, 1991), pp. 354–355.

14. Interview, December 21, 1982. Details concerning Lugar's return from Oxford are also from the July 19, 1991, interview.

15. See Richard Ben Cramer, *What It Takes: The Way to the White House* (New York: Random House, 1992), pp. 360–363. Dukakis finished fifth in the contest to fill four seats, but he was elected in 1959 to the Brookline Town Meeting and in 1960, aged twenty-six, he became chairman of the Brookline Democratic party.

16. Chief Justice John Marshall's opinion in *Marbury v. Madison*, 1 Cranch 137 (1803), established the precedent for judicial review by the U.S. Supreme Court of acts of Congress.

17. Theodore C. Sorenson, *Kennedy* (New York: Bantam Books, 1966), p. 296. (First published, 1965.)
18. Sorenson, *Kennedy,* p. 484.
19. Interview with Paul and Christine Sarbanes, March 3, 1983.
20. Levinson, *Seasons,* pp. 97–101; quotation on p. 99.

CHAPTER 4

Evolving Constituencies
The Political Cultures of Maryland and Indiana

Any representative gains office through election by the constituency and wins reelection by serving it. But what standards guide that service? If constituency opinion were the only influence on senatorial actions, the senator would be the passive instrument of constituency desires. How close do actual senators come to that theoretical passivity? Students of the matter offer a continuum of possible attitudes, from the pure delegate to the pure trustee. A delegate determines and then implements the opinions of his district. A trustee feels that his judgment and knowledge are superior to those of his constituents; he will represent their true interests, but will not be swayed by transient opinions. Edmund Burke's lecture to his constituents is normally cited: "Your representative owes you, not his industry only, but his judgment; and he betrays, instead of serving you, if he sacrifices it to your opinion."[1]

The subjects of social science may also be among its consumers. Both Paul Sarbanes and Richard Lugar volunteered reflections on this presumed dichotomy. Sarbanes thought of it in connection with the six-year term.

> I don't accept this distinction that they're always making, that you're a statesman for three or four years and then you're a candidate for the last two years. It seems to me that you're all of that, sort of rolled up into one, all the time. Like these theories, you know, are you a delegate or a trustee, in terms of how you vote? Either extreme doesn't hold up under analysis, and it seems to me you're always trying to meld the two. I don't want to accept Burke's statement; there's a little too much of "I'll

do what I want," without paying much attention [to the constituents]. But I don't on the other hand accept a kind of weathervane theory. How could you ascertain all their opinions, anyway?[2]

Not long after he entered the Senate, Richard Lugar introduced the same theme.

> You know, hundreds of things float through here. I guess from week to week I can hardly remember what issue we disposed of the week before. We've had 346 roll-call votes thus far this year, and I would guess there are not more than a tenth of those on which there would have been substantial reaction pro or con in Indiana, largely because people were not even aware that such an issue had arisen. On the so-called high profile issues, everybody who has anything to say can be heard . . . I would hope that most of my votes were based on what I believed was genuinely in the public interest.[3]

Thus neither senator is able to operate as a pure delegate, because the issues on which there is a definite and strongly expressed home state opinion are exceptions, but my conversations with them suggest that Lugar is more likely than Sarbanes to see himself on occasion as a Burkean trustee.

The nature of representation is complex. It begins with the reality of constituencies and the human characteristics of representatives. The third element in representation is time. Representation is not a sporadic or discontinuous phenomenon; representation is a process. To understand the actions of Sarbanes and Lugar in the Senate, one must start with the political histories of Maryland and Indiana. How did their political cultures evolve, and what roles do their senior senators play in those cultures?

Maryland: The Assault on Privilege

The story of Maryland's political culture features periodic onslaughts by lesser citizens on the privileges of an entrenched political elite. The story begins with the establishment of a proprietary colony. Under the proprietors, wealth was the avenue to politics; under the bosses of the nineteenth-century Democratic machine, politics became a route to wealth. In the twentieth century, scandals inspired yet another electoral rebellion against the political establishment. Paul Sarbanes, the son of immigrants, has repeated the pattern of Maryland's political history in his own life story.

In 1632, King Charles I granted to George Calvert, the first Lord Baltimore, an area from the headwaters of the Potomac River in the Allegheny Mountains, along the Potomac to where it enters the Chesapeake, then eastward to the Atlantic ocean. The Calverts wished to establish a refuge for persecuted Catholics but knew that Catholics would never constitute a majority of the colony's population. The colonial legislature passed the Toleration Act to ensure religious liberty in 1649. But political and economic power remained in the hands of the wealthy.

The establishment of religious toleration by the Lords Baltimore provided tolerance for the Protestant sects as well as for Catholics, and Jews won the franchise in 1826. Puritanism, such an important part of the New England heritage, found no permanent home in Maryland. The modern version of toleration is more social than religious. The horse racing introduced by the planter elite flourishes in Maryland today. Maryland's attitude toward the Eighteenth Amendment was that the federal government would have to enforce prohibition: it was not a Maryland idea.

Maryland's toleration did not include racial toleration. The first slave was brought into Maryland by the original settlers dispatched by Lord Baltimore. The easy lifestyle of the Tidewater rested on slave labor, and the political culture was long devoted to protecting the slaveholders' advantages. Whites who owned none directed their resentments against the blacks, rather than the slaveowners, repeating the racist tragedy of the American South.

For many Marylanders who fought King George, the battle against England for home rule also concerned who would rule at home.[4] However, the Maryland Constitutional Convention of 1776 was dominated by the planter elite with their professional allies, the lawyers and physicians. The delegates were fervent believers in the English Whig notion that political participation should be limited to those with the greatest "stake in society." Only those owning fifty acres of land, or equivalent movable property, were awarded the franchise. The constitution established property qualifications for holding state offices. Twenty percent of adult white males were eligible for the House of Delegates, 10 percent for the Senate, and only 2 percent for the governorship. Elite control was further assured by a system of selecting members of the legislature by an electoral college in which the centers of greatest population were hardly represented.

When Maryland became the seventh state to ratify the U.S. Constitution, a throng of five thousand celebrated at a picnic on a hill overlooking Baltimore harbor, which has since been known as Federal Hill. Maryland was staunchly Federalist and eagerly ceded land for the establishment of the national capital on the Potomac.

An era of national expansion and speculation followed the Revolution. The National Road, one of Thomas Jefferson's visions, was planned in 1806, and construction began in 1811 at Cumberland, Maryland. It became the main wagon passage over the Alleghenies into the Ohio Valley. Baltimore rivaled New York and Philadelphia as the center for trade between the new West and Europe.

When Southern states began to secede from the Union upon the election of Abraham Lincoln, attention centered on the slaveholding border states. If Maryland joined the Confederacy, the national capital would be cut off from the Union. Maryland loyalties were sharply divided, but Union sympathizers, backed by the Union Army, prevented secession. In 1862, Robert E. Lee invaded western Maryland, trying to isolate Washington, Baltimore, and Philadelphia and thus end the war. He was halted at the two-day battle of Antietam Creek. A similar drive in 1863 ended at Gettysburg, Pennsylvania. The possibility of Southern victory through invasion of the North was ended.

Civil War loyalties endured for generations in Maryland politics. In 1867, the Tidewater counties became Democratic; but it was the Whig party of the old slave owners under a new name, still the party of white supremacy. The foreign-stock workers of Baltimore were also Democrats, but they were organized by a different kind of party, based on strong ethnic neighborhoods. The Democratic machine controlled the state from 1867 until 1912, with only a five-year Republican interlude, and the machine was controlled for thirty years by I. Freeman Rasin and Arthur Pue Gorman. Serving modestly as clerk of the Court of Common Pleas, Rasin was the boss of Baltimore, while Gorman managed the rest of the state, eventually from a seat in the U.S. Senate.[5]

Republican farmers in the Piedmont and Appalachian areas had opposed slavery and remained as loyal to the party of abolition as did the freedmen. Western Maryland developed a vigorous two-party system, with the Democrats supported by miners and working men, but the area contained only a minority of the state's voters. The problem for Gorman and Rasin was to nominate candidates who would be supported in Baltimore without alienating the Tidewater, and particularly the Eastern Shore. Maryland seemed a part of the solid Democratic South as long as the Democratic leaders could hold their voters together. When the Democrats split, progressive Republicans could triumph, as they did in 1912. The Republicans of western Maryland remain today more liberal than the national party.

The New Deal modified the three-part structure of Maryland politics. The Baltimore Democrats became more responsive to organized labor. Black voters switched their allegiance from the Republican to the Democratic party. Democrats still had to placate the Tidewater Bourbons to defeat the liberal Republicans of Western Maryland, so the party remained conservative. President Franklin D. Roosevelt's attempt at ideological streamlining of the Democratic party took the form, in Maryland, of supporting a campaign against U.S. senator Millard Tydings, running for a third term in 1938. Tydings played upon the resentment of outside interference. He won easily and was reelected to a fourth term in 1944.

Tidewater whites turned toward the Republicans when the Democratic party embraced integration and the black vote. However, the population growth of the region has been modest, compared to the rest of the state. One of Maryland's eight congressional districts serves the entire Eastern Shore and leaps the Chesapeake to include the state capital, Annapolis, and some affluent suburbs. The area gave birth to Maryland's political culture, but its influence has faded away.

Dramatic population growth came to seven suburban counties—five counties surrounding Baltimore City and two counties bordering the District of Columbia that are heavily populated by federal employees. By 1960, 75 percent of Maryland's population lived in these suburbs; they elected only half the delegates to the General Assembly and 30 percent of the legislature's upper house. In the familiar Maryland pattern, established elites fiercely resisted suburbanite demands for fair representation. Their resistance ended in 1964 when the U.S. Supreme Court ordered the reapportionment of both houses of Maryland's legislature.[6]

Spiro T. Agnew became the suburbanites' champion. He was initially elected the Executive of Baltimore County, a separate area north of the city of Baltimore, due to a split in the local Democrats. Agnew was unsure of election for a second term, so he ran for governor in 1966 against Democrat George P. Mahoney. Mahoney was perennially favored by the Ku Klux Klan, so Agnew, perceived as the candidate with more respectable views on racial matters, was elected. Two years later, Richard Nixon named Agnew as his running mate, hoping to consolidate the Republican hold on the suburbs. When the press revealed that he accepted payoffs from Maryland contractors even while occupying the vice president's office, Agnew resigned. The challenge of building a responsive majority party in Maryland passed to the Democrats.

That challenge was already confronted by a group of younger Democrats in East Baltimore, including Paul Sarbanes, who built their own alternatives to the traditional patronage-oriented coalitions. The reformers' greatest obstacles were officeholders in the state administration. Marvin Mandel had risen through the traditional Democratic organization to become Speaker of the House of Delegates. When Governor Agnew resigned to become vice president, Mandel was elected by the Democratic legislature to complete Agnew's term. Paul Sarbanes voted against him. Mandel readily won election on his own right in 1970. In November 1975, Governor Mandel was indicted by a federal grand jury for accepting bribes from his five closest friends. That fact was not disputed, but proving that Mandel did favors in return was much more difficult. Mandel was convicted of mail fraud in December of 1976.

Mandel's case was the culmination of political scandals which made Maryland seem the corruption capital of the nation. Among those indicted were two successive governors, two congressmen, the Speaker of the House of Delegates, eight other members of the General Assembly, and fourteen major county and state officials. But these cases were only marginally related to each other. An epitaph for the era was written by George Callcott.

> Each Maryland politician was operating mostly on his own, accepting favors and providing them in the way many assumed politics was supposed to work . . . Patronage held the party workers together; large favors to the rich brought campaign contributions and small personal favors to the poor brought votes . . . Suburbanites and bureaucrats wanted government not of favors but of impersonal rules that applied alike to all . . . The old politics was based on favors. The new politics was based on the assumption that favors were corrupt.[7]

Paul Sarbanes was a leading practitioner of the new Democratic politics. Building on his base in the Greek community, he campaigned from door to door to build a following that was more personal than partisan. In 1970, he was elected to the U.S. House of Representatives. In 1976, he won the U.S. Senate seat. The election of Paul Sarbanes, son of Greek immigrants, symbolized the arrival of the new politics.

Maryland's contemporary political culture developed in step with the modernization of the state's Democratic party. Final repudiation of the machine-style politics developed in the nineteenth century came fairly late, with the "last hurrah" of Marvin Mandel. The party had to overcome the taint of corruption; the task was made easier because Spiro Agnew's Republicans were similarly tainted. At the same time, the party was adapting to the civil rights revolution, which assured access to the ballot, for the first time, to all strata of Maryland society. The Democrats labored to encompass the attitudes of the burgeoning suburbs. As political institutions became open to all, and welfare functions were performed by government, the party withered as a separate organization and hierarchy. The party's elected officeholders became its leaders. The day of unelected party bosses was over. Candidates came to depend on personal organizations that supplanted the established party.

Paul Sarbanes' political career spanned the era of these adaptations. As a second-generation immigrant, his own life repeated the newcomers' campaign against established privilege that is the theme of Maryland's political history. In becoming a senator, however, he became a member of the state's political establishment and a target for the ambitions of others. Although he faces no serious assault from members of his own party, Maryland's Republicans have mounted lively, but usually underfinanced, campaigns against him.

Indiana: Old-Fashioned Parties

Even as the delegates in Philadelphia debated provisions of a new United States Constitution, the Continental Congress, meeting in New York, established conditions for the admission of new states from the area northwest of the Ohio River. The Northwest Ordinance of 1787 assured religious liberty and civil rights for the settlers, allotted public lands to finance education, and excluded slavery.

The Ohio Valley became American when the Revolutionary War ended. The federal government's policy was to purchase Indian lands, but Americans did not wait for this formality to claim the frontier. The Indians rallied to protect their territory; raids on the settlers stimulated a military response. General William Henry Harrison, governor of the Indiana Territory, emerged as a hero of these conflicts.

Indiana's first constitution institutionalized frontier equality. After visiting America in 1840, Count Alexis de Tocqueville wrote that a unique feature of the Americans was that they were "born equal."[8] Feudalism never existed here, so revolutionary effort was not required to establish the principle of equality. Had he visited Indiana, the French aristocrat could have exhibited the Hoosiers to demonstrate his point, just as the Maryland experience somewhat contradicted it. There were no property qualifications for voting or officeholding in Indiana, and there were no elites determined to exclude other white citizens from economic or political participation. Indiana residents achieved a common identity as "Hoosiers." Appearing in print as early as 1830, the term carried a rustic connotation and included shrewdness, along with "conservatism and steadfastness and common sense."[9]

One of the surveyors who platted the new capital city of Indianapolis was Alexander Ralston, who assisted Pierre L'Enfant in planning the District of Columbia. Ralston laid out a four-acre circle for the city's center. Eight wide thoroughfares radiated from it. The circle came into its glory only in 1902, when a monument was completed to the enlisted ranks of the Civil War. Monument Circle remains the focal point of government and commerce in Indianapolis.

Thomas Jefferson's National Road, which began in Cumberland, Maryland, reached Monument Circle in 1830. The road established a line through the center of the state which became U.S. Highway 40 and is now I–70. It is the dividing line between two Indianas. South of the line, settlers came from the slaveholding states of the South. Even today, their speech suggests a Southern drawl. North of the National Road, immigrants came a few years later by way of Ohio or Pennsylvania from New England or Europe. The accents of northern Indiana have the flat As and hard Rs of the Midwest.

The Whig party named William Henry Harrison as their presidential candidate. Whigs won local offices in Indiana in 1836, although Harrison lost the White House to Martin Van Buren. In the "log cabin and hard cider" rerun of 1840, Whig editors described the old Virginia aristocrat as the product of humble origins.

Apart from a five-day, two-hundred-mile raid by Confederate cavalry north of the Ohio River, no Civil War battles were fought within Indiana's borders. But the state contributed 197,000 Union troops from a prewar population of 1.3 million. The war created a permanent division between Republicans, north of the old national road, and Democrats to the south.

Republicans and Democrats alternated in the state government and in Congress. The geographical partisan division brought victory to the organization best able to turn out its adherents, and "the cost of a vote in Indianapolis in 1876 was ten dollars."[10] The outcome in Indiana became crucial to the national political contest. The state supplied five vice presidents, and Indianapolis Republican lawyer Benjamin Harrison (grandson of the first President Harrison) won the White House in 1888.

While the bucolic Indiana of song and story celebrates rural pleasures—think of James Whitcomb Riley's poetry and the popularity of Nashville music with contemporary Hoosiers—the state has been industrialized since the 1850s. A generation of eager inventors and entrepreneurs, including Richard Lugar's grandfather, built Indiana as a major manufacturing center during the Gilded Age. Indiana gave birth to the automobile industry when Elwood Haynes of Kokomo built the first successful clutch-driven, spark-ignition auto in 1893.

Manufacturers needed steel. In 1906, the United States Steel Corporation founded the city of Gary on the shore of Lake Michigan and built the nation's largest steel mills. The mills attracted a labor force of immigrants from Eastern Europe and, later, blacks from the American South. Lake County, in the northwest corner of Indiana, developed a culture like that of Chicago and a politics based on social class. It became an enclave in a state divided by Civil War animosities.

With economic collapse, Indiana turned to the opposition party. In 1932, Democrat Paul V. McNutt was elected the first of three Democratic governors. He joined the Roosevelt administration and sought the 1940 presidential nomination. His efforts made progress, until Franklin D. Roosevelt claimed a third term. The 1940 Republican nominee was a native Hoosier transplanted to Wall Street, utility magnate Wendell Willkie.

World War II brought the state $7 billion in defense contracts and a new influx of workers. By the 1970s, Indiana led the nation in the manufacture of steel and was second only to Michigan in making automobiles. Ten percent of the population was classified as "farm" and only 3 percent of the state's work force was employed in agriculture; yet central Indiana contains some of the richest farm land in the nation, with corn and hogs the leading products. Much of the state's industrial activity centers on producing farm supplies and equipment, so the economic health of agriculture profoundly affects Indiana's prosperity.

After 1944, Indiana's influence in presidential politics seemed at an end. Its image became one of rural, conservative Republicanism. Charles Halleck provided able party leadership in the House of Representatives, while U.S. Senator William Jenner was an apostle of isolationist, McCarthyite Republicanism from 1947 to 1959 and "ran the GOP in Indiana for most of the years from 1945 to 1960."[11]

The state was changing. Even as the ultraconservative John Birch Society was being founded in Indianapolis in 1958, Democrat R. Vance Hartke defeated Jenner for the United States Senate seat. Democrat Matthew Welsh became governor in 1960; in 1962, thirty-four-year-old Birch Bayh upset stalwart Republican Homer Capehart to join Hartke in the Senate. In 1965, a Democratic legislature repealed Indiana's right-to-work law.

With Jenner-style Republicanism rejected at the polls, a group of younger party members began to rebuild the organization in Indianapolis. They sought candidates who would give the party a more vital image. Richard Lugar's entry into partisan politics was claimed as a success of the recruitment effort; Lugar's ambition no doubt made him a willing recruit.

Indiana political contests have not been over the structure of society but over who should operate the governmental machinery. More than any other state, Indiana remains true to the Jacksonian heritage of the spoils system. Until the practice was abolished in 1988, organizational strength was based on the "2 percent club"—officials placed in office by their party contributed 2 percent of their salaries to the organization. Since the party losing the governorship can still count on staffing many county court houses, both parties have secure bases, and they cooperate to preserve the system. Upper level professional positions in state government are recommended by bipartisan, rather than nonpartisan, commissions. The strength of the two parties has meant that an opposition was always ready to displace the incumbents when the electorate tired of corruption or incompetence, or simply grew bored with familiar faces.

The influence of party leaders on nominations for statewide office was assured by making them in state conventions. Half a century after abolishing statewide primaries to limit Ku Klux Klan influence, Indiana returned to primaries in 1976. The Republican legislature felt that Democratic voters would renominate incumbent U.S. Senator Vance Hartke, but a Democratic convention would surely dump Hartke for a stronger candidate. Dick Lugar was the Republican organization's candidate for the Senate, and he beat Hartke easily.

Indiana's political culture began in the heyday of Jacksonian frontier equality and quickly developed two vital parties. Geographical divisions between the parties established by the Civil War remain important. Except for the area around Gary, Indiana was basically settled by the Civil War's end. When the Ku Klux Klan marched against Catholics and Jews in the 1920s, these enemies were largely of the imagination; there were few adherents of either religion in central Indiana. In 1980, Indiana's black population totaled only 7 percent, compared to 21 percent in Maryland. A relatively stable population has meant that Indiana politics has changed less than in other states because Indiana life has changed less. "This is a state not far from the more innocent America of barbershop quartets and ice cream socials."[12]

Indiana never really repudiated machine-style politics. Some of its features have been abolished by one party or the other to achieve short-term advantage. The Republicans reestablished primary elections to make nominations for statewide office in 1976; twelve years later, a Democratic candidate attacked the 2 percent clubs. Political culture in Indiana begins to look, on the surface, more like that in other states, and these changes will inevitably weaken its party organizations.

Two Senators and Their States

Maryland and Indiana are alike in having relatively small areas with fairly dense populations. Their populations are comparable; Indiana has some 900,000 more than Maryland's 5 million. Both have been border states, positioned between the different political convictions of North and South. One difference is that Indiana's political season is longer. Hoosier primaries are held in the spring of election years, a legacy of the time when politics was the main summer entertainment of rural Indiana. Maryland waits until the fall.

Maryland has changed from the conservative politics of a proprietary colony to the liberal outlook of a diverse and tolerant population. Senators Paul Sarbanes and Barbara Mikulski are counted as liberal, northern Democrats. Half a century ago, Maryland senators were counted as southern and conservative. Liberalism found a home in the Maryland Republican party, in such figures as former governor Theodore Roosevelt McKeldin and ex-senator Charles Mathias. In 1964, Barry Goldwater called for the defeat of liberals in the national Republican party; in the 1970s, Spiro Agnew chose racism and an anti-hippie crusade for the Maryland Republicans. The Maryland Democratic party cut its ties to the traditional white supremacist attitudes of the Tidewater and responded to the needs of blacks and suburbanites, becoming the state's unchallenged majority party.

For the last decade and a half, Maryland has been a liberal, Democratic state, but there have been changes in its liberalism. Barbara Mikulski partly represents the influence of the feminist left among Maryland Democrats, which was unknown in the 1970s.

Indiana was born in Jacksonian populism, matured with a nonideological two-party system, and has returned to the bipartisan conservative outlook that sustained the state nearly a century ago. Republicans and Democrats have alternated in office, almost on a generational basis. Richard Lugar was perfectly positioned to ride the 1970s Republican tide into the U.S. Senate. But change has come again in Indiana politics. A Democratic governor was elected in 1988 (partly because his policies were more conservative than those of the Republican incumbent.) The Christian right has won new influence in the Indiana Republican party, as it has in the nation. Yet Lugar has been elected four times to the Senate, with increasing majorities.

Their different constituencies partially explain the contrasting records of Senators Sarbanes and Lugar. In this account, the critical episodes are the reversals of fortune in which the electorate replaces an incumbent party or officeholder. Such a dramatic display of electoral power is the exception, not the rule, because incumbents of both parties tend to be experienced and responsive politicians. The constituency influences senatorial choice every day, not only during election campaigns.

How may the constituency's impact between campaigns be measured? Even if there were a valid survey of public opinion on every issue, we cannot enter the senatorial mind to learn whether the poll results tipped the balance of decision. We do have an intriguing chance for comparison, since every state is represented by two senators. Lugar and Sarbanes entered the Senate together in 1977; consider their senior colleagues. Liberal Democrat Sarbanes joined liberal Republican Charles Mathias in the Senate, and Mathias was reelected in 1982, so Sarbanes remained Maryland's junior senator for ten years. Conservative Republican Lugar joined liberal Democrat Birch Bayh, but Bayh was soon defeated, and Lugar remained the junior senator for only four years.

When states are represented by both Republican and Democratic senators, their votes may cancel each other, except when determining issues on which both senators perceive an actual or potential intense opinion, or a clearly affected state interest, or the parties have avoided taking a position on the question. Senators' choices are declared and recorded publicly. For many years, the *Congressional Quarterly* organization has published studies of three dimensions of roll-call voting from which one may infer the nature of influences on voting. The first is the index of party unity, which tallies all votes on which majorities of the two parties were opposed—votes on which party made a difference. The index provides the percentage of votes that an individual cast to support, or to oppose, the majority of his partisan colleagues. When the percentage of votes supporting the party is high, one may infer that the senator agrees with the party position, or that he thinks that his constituents agree with the party position, or both.

The second index measures presidential support. How did the senator vote on measures publicly supported by the president? The president's position may be a central ingredient of the political context at the point of choice. If the president is extremely popular within his state, the senator will prepare a careful explanation of why he voted against the president on a major issue.

The third index encourages inference about the importance of ideology. It is based on the votes in which a majority of Republicans join with a majority of southern Democrats to form the conservative coalition. Sixty years ago, the coalition formed frequently and was a dominant force. So many conservative southern jurisdictions now elect Republicans that the conservative coalition forms less frequently, but it often carries the day. A high percentage of support for the conservative coalition suggests a conservative ideology.

Table 4–1 gives these three indexes for the Maryland senators for the last twenty years. Note that Senator Mathias opposed the Republican majority more frequently than he supported it during eight of the ten years after 1977. He habitually opposed the conservative coalition, and he supported Democratic president Jimmy Carter more faithfully than Republican Ronald Reagan. Nevertheless, during the ten years they both represented Maryland, Mathias's voting record never approached Sarbanes' partisan Democratic liberalism. Mathias was a respected member of an old Maryland family with roots in western Maryland's liberal Republican territory. He was not defeated in 1986; he declined to seek reelection.

Before 1976, both Indiana senators were Democrats. When Dick Lugar first ran for the Senate in 1974 against Birch Bayh, he was narrowly defeated. Two years later, he ran against the other Democratic incumbent, Vance Hartke, and was elected easily. If the constituency were the main determining factor, one would expect convergence, rather than divergence, in the voting records of Democrat Bayh and Republican Lugar. Table 4–2 shows that, in 1977 and 1978, Bayh was as partisan a Democrat as Lugar was a dedicated Republican.

For the final two years of his term, with the reelection campaign looming, Bayh's support for the Democratic majority fell by some 20 percent, and his support for President Carter declined by an average of 16 percent. Bayh supported only 5 percent of conservative coalition votes in 1977—his score was a mirror image of Lugar's—but his support for the coalition rose

TABLE 4–1

Party Unity, Presidential Support, and Conservative Coalition Voting Scores for the Senators from Maryland, 1977–1996

Year		Party Unity		Pres. Support		Cons. Coalition	
		Unity	Oppn.	Supp.	Oppn.	Supp.	Oppn.
				CARTER			
1977	Mathias (R)	25	60	64	19	30	60
	Sarbanes (D)	92	6	82	17	4	94
1978	Mathias	16	65	66	10	16	69
	Sarbanes	94	5	87	12	6	91
1979	Mathias	23	66	73	16	22	71
	Sarbanes	88	10	85	12	8	91
1980	Mathias	16	55	48	17	10	61
	Sarbanes	87	11	73	25	4	92
				REAGAN			
1981	Mathias	44	34	58	27	26	48
	Sarbanes	93	6	38	61	7	93
1982	Mathias	39	50	51	38	33	57
	Sarbanes	91	3	25	65	2	78
1983	Mathias	40	41	60	26	32	55
	Sarbanes	88	9	41	58	11	84
1984	Mathias	52	39	51	42	49	49
	Sarbanes	94	2	30	64	0	98
1985	Mathias	33	51	43	44	28	58
	Sarbanes	90	5	22	74	8	87
1986	Mathias	31	55	36	52	26	62
	Sarbanes	96	3	18	81	3	95
1987	Sarbanes (D)	95	4	31	67	6	94
	Mikulski (D)	93	4	28	64	13	84
1988	Sarbanes	96	4	40	59	8	92
	Mikulski	93	3	40	58	5	92
				BUSH			
1989	Sarbanes	95	4	45	53	11	87
	Mikulski	94	5	41	56	11	89
1990	Sarbanes	93	7	31	69	11	89
	Mikulski	89	11	26	73	16	81

(continued)

TABLE 4–1 (*continued*)

Year		Party Unity		Pres. Support		Cons. Coalition	
		Unity	Oppn.	Supp.	Oppn.	Supp.	Oppn.
1991	Sarbanes	96	4	30	70	13	88
	Mikulski	91	8	33	67	33	65
1992	Sarbanes	96	4	27	73	11	89
	Mikulski	87	10	23	77	24	74
				CLINTON			
1993	Sarbanes	98	2	96	4	12	88
	Mikulski	92	8	93	4	39	64
1994	Sarbanes	98	2	95	5	13	88
	Mikulski	89	9	89	6	28	69
1995	Sarbanes	95	4	90	10	9	89
	Mikulski	82	12	85	11	33	56
1996	Sarbanes	94	6	90	10	18	82
	Mikulski	92	8	90	10	32	68

Source: *Congressional Quarterly Almanac*, 1977–1996

to 21 percent in 1980. Apparently opinion trends in Indiana moved Senator Bayh's votes, modestly but significantly, in Senator Lugar's direction.

These data confirm that Lugar and Sarbanes were in the vanguard of political movements in their respective states; Maryland was becoming a Democratic state, while Indiana's trend was conservative and Republican. This conclusion, reached by comparing Sarbanes and Lugar with their predecessors, is reinforced by considering the persons elected to the Senate by their states in 1980, when Lugar became Indiana's senior senator, in 1986, when Sarbanes became the senior senator from Maryland, and in 1988, when Indiana elected a new junior senator.

In Indiana, as in the nation, 1980 was a year of high interest rates and increasing unemployment, coupled with a sense of national frustration as Iran held American hostages. A young Indiana congressman, Dan Quayle, challenged Senator Birch Bayh and won. Ronald Reagan won the White House, and Republicans captured a slender majority of the Senate. Dan Quayle described his campaign to Richard Fenno:

> You had a classic contest between two philosophies, and the people want a conservative philosophy . . . We stuck to one theme—that 300,000 people were without jobs and that Birch Bayh was to blame.[13]

TABLE 4-2

Party Unity, Presidential Support, and Conservative Coalition Scores for the Senators from Indiana, 1977–1996

Year		Party Unity		Pres. Support		Cons. Coalition	
		Unity	Oppn.	Supp.	Oppn.	Supp.	Oppn.
		CARTER					
1977	Bayh (D)	83%	10%	73%	20%	5%	90%
	Lugar (R)	91	8	48	51	95	4
1978	Bayh	83	9	74	14	14	78
	Lugar	85	14	35	64	80	20
1979	Bayh	63	9	61	20	16	58
	Lugar	90	10	43	57	90	10
1980	Bayh	61	15	54	22	21	57
	Lugar	80	12	44	53	85	10
		REAGAN					
1981	Lugar (R)	93	7	90	9	90	10
	Quayle (R)	93	6	87	13	88	8
1982	Lugar	85	14	83	15	84	16
	Quayle	87	12	84	15	86	14
1983	Lugar	92	8	95	5	95	5
	Quayle	85	11	88	7	86	5
1984	Lugar	94	6	92	8	87	13
	Quayle	90	8	86	12	81	15
1985	Lugar	92	8	89	10	88	12
	Quayle	93	5	88	11	90	10
1986	Lugar	89	10	88	11	88	9
	Quayle	94	5	90	8	95	3
1987	Lugar	77	20	76	21	78	13
	Quayle	89	9	71	27	88	9
1988	Lugar	76	19	86	13	86	14
	Quayle	79	3	73	17	84	5
		BUSH					
1989	Lugar (R)	83	15	93	2	84	11
	Coats (R)	92	8	81	19	92	8
1990	Lugar	86	12	86	11	97	3
	Coats	87	11	77	18	92	8

(continued)

TABLE 4–2 (*continued*)

Year		Party Unity		Pres. Support		Cons. Coalition	
		Unity	Oppn.	Supp.	Oppn.	Supp.	Oppn.
1991	Lugar	88	11	93	7	83	10
	Coats	91	9	85	15	85	15
1992	Lugar	86	12	87	10	76	21
	Coats	92	8	75	22	87	13
	CLINTON						
1993	Lugar	88	12	30	65	88	10
	Coats	78	22	29	70	80	20
1994	Lugar	78	22	45	55	78	22
	Coats	88	11	42	58	78	19
1995	Lugar	88	7	26	67	79	16
	Coats	97	2	23	76	95	5
1996	Lugar	88	10	31	68	92	8
	Coats	93	4	29	68	84	11

Source: *Congressional Quarterly Almanac, 1977–1996*

A map of the 1980 Senate vote shows Bayh carrying half the counties below the old National Road, while Quayle carried all but four of the counties to the north—"a result eerily similar to that of 1868."[14] In the vanguard of reborn Republican conservatism, Richard Lugar seemingly anticipated an ideological victory confirmed in Indiana by Dan Quayle and in the nation by Ronald Reagan. Quayle's voting record in the Senate was very similar to Lugar's from 1981 to 1986. Their records diverged thereafter, as Quayle voted with the Republican majority somewhat more frequently than Lugar.

When Dan Quayle served in the House of Representatives, Dan Coats served him as a key staff member. Coats is credited with introducing Quayle to the organized Christian Right in Indiana. When Quayle moved up to the Senate in 1980, Coats won the House seat. In 1988, Quayle was elected as President George Bush's running mate; Coats was appointed to the Senate seat and won it in his own right in 1992. As a dedicated Christian conservative, Coats has been more in tune than Dick Lugar with the new Republican party. Their scores diverged markedly after 1994, when the new Republicans helped win a majority in the House of Representatives. Lugar scored a mere 64 percent in the ratings of the Christian Coalition, compared to Coats's 100 percent. In December 1996, Coats announced that he would not seek reelection in 1998. "I want to leave," he stated, "while there is still a chance to follow God's leading to something new."[15]

Voter reaction to the 1994 conservative triumph was very different in Maryland. Both Maryland senators won zeros on the Christian Coalition scoreboard. Maryland has become one of the nation's most Democratic states: one of only six states to vote for Jimmy Carter in 1980, it awarded a slender 51 percent of its vote to Bush in 1988. Paul Sarbanes is listed as a northern, liberal Democrat. Maryland's Democrats became the contemporary majority by voicing the concerns of both the burgeoning suburbs and the growing black population; Paul Sarbanes led the way. In 1974, Barbara Mikulski came from her Baltimore Polish neighborhood to run against Senator Charles Mathias; she lost by 7 percent. In 1976, she won the Third District Congressional seat being vacated by Paul Sarbanes. In 1986, when Mathias retired, she won the Senate seat easily, following the political trail Sarbanes blazed. Her voting record in the Senate has followed Paul Sarbanes' record very closely, although Sarbanes has been slightly more faithful to the Senate Democratic party. Senator Mikulski has been more aggressive in taking positions, particularly on family and feminist issues.

Lugar and Sarbanes were elected to the Senate in 1976 and reelected in 1982 as leaders of the ascendant political sentiment in their respective states. Ironically, one of the benefits of winning by a large majority is the sense of greater freedom to exercise personal judgment without the fear of marginal changes in constituent opinion. Yet the legislator achieves that majority, in large measure, by building trust among constituents, persuading them that she or he remains in touch with their interests and desires. Choices seem more free today because they were constrained yesterday.

Notes

1. See Burke's "Speech to the Electors of Bristol," *Writings and Speeches of Edmund Burke* (Boston: Little, Brown, 1901), vol. 2, pp. 93–98. Quoted in David J. Vogler, *The Politics of Congress* (Boston: Allyn and Bacon, 1983), p. 76.
2. Interview with Senator Sarbanes, July 5, 1982.
3. Quoted from the author's interview with then freshman Senator Lugar in September 1977. I have described this interview, as well as interviews with 116 other political influentials, including Paul Sarbanes, in *The Guardians: Leadership Values and the American Tradition* (New York: Norton, 1982).
4. The sentence is paraphrased from Jesse Lemisch's "The Revolution Seen from the Bottom Up," in B.J. Berstein, ed., *Towards a New Past: Dissenting Essays in American History* (New York: Pantheon Books, 1967), p. 19, quoted in David Curtin Skaggs, *Roots of Maryland Democracy: 1753–1776* (Westport, Conn:

Greenwood Press, 1973), p. 8. My description of the political setting of Maryland's first constitution is based on Skaggs' account.

5. For an account of the antics of Gorman and Rasin, see Carl Bode, *Maryland: A Bicentennial History* (New York: Norton, 1978), pp. 134–147. A contemporary account is Frank Kent, *The Story of Maryland Politics* (Baltimore: Thomas and Evans Printing Co., 1911), which depicts political conflicts from 1864 to 1910. Also see John R. Lambert, *Arthur Pue Gorman* (Baton Rouge: Louisiana State University Press, 1953).

6. *Maryland Committee for Fair Representation v. Tawes*, 377 U.S. 656.

7. George H. Callcott, *Maryland and America, 1940 to 1980* (Baltimore: Johns Hopkins University Press, 1985) pp. 297, 299.

8. *Democracy in America*, tr. Henry Reeve, 2 vols. (New York: Schocken Books, 1961), II, p. 122.

9. John Bartlow Martin, *Indiana: An Interpretation* (New York: Alfred A. Knopf, 1947), p. 269.

10. Martin, *Indiana: An Interpretation*, pp. 76, 102.

11. Edward H. Ziegner in Donald F. Carmony, ed., *Indiana: A Self Appraisal* (Bloomington: Indiana University Press, 1966), p. 53.

12. Michael Barone and Grant Ujifusa, *The Almanac of American Politics 1990* (Washington, D.C.: National Journal, 1989), p. 396.

13. Richard F. Fenno, Jr., *The Making of a Senator: Dan Quayle* (Washington, D.C.: Congressional Quarterly Press, 1989), p. 19.

14. *The Almanac of American Politics, 1990*, p. 396.

15. *The Almanac of American Politics, 1998*, p. 525.

CHAPTER 5

Apprenticeships

Party Support and Political Styles

The authors of the American Constitution realized that democratic logic permits few limitations on the public's choice. The only qualifications they specified for senators are that "he" (the gender limitation was assumed) shall be thirty years of age, nine years a citizen of the United States, and, at the time of election, "an inhabitant of the state for which he shall be chosen." There is still no prescribed method for training a prospective senator. More than a century ago, Woodrow Wilson wrote:

> There cannot be a separate breed of public men reared especially for the Senate. It must be recruited from the lower branches of the representative system . . . [T]hough it may not be as good as one wished, the Senate is as good as it can be under the circumstances. It contains the most perfect product of our politics, whatever that product may be.[1]

The direct election of U.S. senators, provided in 1913 by Amendment XVII, gave new freedom to the public choice. But the parties and the voters did not choose strangers. Candidates normally win election to the Senate after testing in lesser elective office. Like most of their Senate colleagues, Paul Sarbanes and Richard Lugar served significant apprenticeships. In these positions, they perfected their political styles. A key element of the political style is the representative's habitual manner of self-presentation to the constituency as well as to fellow legislators. Their apprenticeship positions reinforced Lugar's tendency to turn first to rhetoric as a tool of influence and Sarbanes' preference for close, personal contact with both constituents and fellow legislators. A second result of their apprenticeship was to establish habits of working within their parties, as each discovered the kinds of support he could count on from the party. Dick Lugar found the party's help particularly welcome, since his first elected office was strictly nonpartisan, unpaid, and provided him no staff support.

School Issues Awaken Indianapolis

In the fall of 1963, after four years of intense effort, business successes promised eventually to allow the Lugar brothers to pay their debts. Dick Lugar's interest in international politics, so stimulated by working for Admiral Burke, had not lapsed, but he did not seek immediate involvement.

Local involvement sought him. Lugar was invited to become the candidate from the west side of Indianapolis on a slate of seven candidates to be put forward by the Citizens' School Committee for election to the Board of School Commissioners in 1964. The Citizens' Committee recruits had always enjoyed an advantage in the nonpartisan election because school commissioners were elected at large by the entire city. Independent candidates with only a neighborhood following had little chance; racial minorities were not represented.

This time, the mostly Republican Citizen's Committee slate could not coast to an easy victory. They were faced by an opposing coalition of labor and civil rights groups, called Non-Partisans for Better Schools, consisting mostly of Democrats. Lugar was caught up in a full-fledged campaign, with television debates, brochures distributed door to door, and the other trappings of a partisan contest. Lugar's earnest but fluent debating style made him something of a local television celebrity, and he won the second largest vote total; some candidates from each slate were elected.

No part of the Indianapolis city government had ever accepted aid from the federal government. This stance was approved by the chamber of commerce and the industrial elite and was practiced by both parties when they held city hall. Public school issues first led Indianapolis to confront the changed social realities of the 1960s. In 1954, the U.S. Supreme Court declared racial segregation in the public schools to be unconstitutional.[2] The decision was not self-enforcing. Lugar's old high school, Shortridge, lily white in the early 1950s, had a 91 percent black student body in 1964. Would the school board dare implement the Supreme Court decision by assigning white students to a black high school?

Dick Lugar cast the determining vote for the city to enroll in the school lunch program and to accept the federal aid available under the Education Act. Lugar became the principal advocate of the Shortridge Plan, which proposed returning Shortridge to its former status as the city's elite college preparatory high school, a magnet to attract students from all areas. A 4–3 majority of the board approved the plan. Shortridge High enrolled a 52 percent white freshmen class in the fall of 1965; voluntary school integration seemed a real possibility. Then came the backlash. Other high schools complained that their best students were being "skimmed" by Shortridge. The black community was divided. Some saw the plan as a genuine promise of racial comity in Indianapolis. Others blacks feared they were losing "their" high school. In July 1966, new members joined the board. In 1991, Lugar described the new majority of 1966.

> They were under some head of steam that these experiments in voluntary desegregation were leading to some problems. The sadness is that the reaction was, in my judgment, a very very ham-handed one, in which they simply said, "Enough of . . . all this stuff." As a result, the NAACP then filed suit, the school system went into court within a year and stays there to this day.[3]

At that point, Lugar was approached by Keith Buhlen, who was rebuilding the Republican organization as Marion County chairman. Buhlen persuaded Lugar to serve as campaign chairman for the city's Republican congressional candidate. The main responsibility of the campaign chairman was to speak on the candidate's behalf when overlapping obligations made it impossible for the candidate to attend particular functions. The contest itself was hopeless, as the Democratic incumbent was well entrenched, but Lugar got acquainted with the Republican organization, and they came to know him, above all, as a public speaker. In 1967, Buhlen asked Lugar to become the organization's candidate for mayor of Indianapolis. Buhlen invited a test of his own leadership, since Alex Clark, the last Republican to serve as mayor, sixteen years before, hoped to recapture the office from the Democratic incumbent. While Clark was very popular with Republicans, the GOP was in a minority in the city, and Buhlen felt Clark had no chance in the general election. With the help of Buhlen's revitalized organization, Lugar won the primary easily. He then waged an intensive five-month campaign to win the general election by nine thousand votes.

The Making of Modern Indianapolis

The new mayor's first act, after inauguration on January 1, 1968, was to close the city's fourteen open, burning refuse dumps and to substitute, with great fanfare, a system of sanitary landfills. This tribute to ecological consciousness was arranged in advance. Other projects were developed by Republican Committeemen—unsafe pavements, crumbled curbs, dangerous corners needing traffic lights, and many other urban needs—until there was a priority list of 192 necessary projects.

Keith Buhlen recalled that it required nearly all of Lugar's first term to accomplish the 192 projects, and a major newspaper criticized the role of party officials in setting the priorities—service should be available to any citizen, without concern for party. Buhlen saw the party organization as far more responsive and responsible than any civil service bureaucracy; patronage workers know that the party must win reelection for them to retain their jobs.[4]

The projects list was barely formulated when Mayor Lugar faced the local manifestation of a national crisis. It began on his own thirty-sixth birthday, April 4, 1968. Lyndon Johnson had withdrawn from the contest for the Democratic presidential nomination. The first test between Robert Kennedy and Eugene McCarthy would be the Indiana primary on April 7. The mayor's office had spent most of April 4 arranging security for Kennedy, who was bringing his campaign to Indianapolis that evening.

Lugar was attending a banquet when a police officer brought him word that Dr. Martin Luther King, Jr., had been killed. The news of King's death was flashed around the world as Kennedy was arriving at a campaign rally, but it had not reached the audience. Kennedy climbed onto a flatbed truck in a parking lot, under a stand of oak trees. He had to begin by announcing the death of Martin Luther King. Then he made a moving, impromptu statement. Dick Lugar recalled the event.

> It was one of the remarkable moments in history, Kennedy's speech, in which he mentioned Euripides . . . It was played again and again, at the Democratic National Convention and then in USIA films. It was a magnificent statement, to a shocked group of people there that night.

After seeing Robert Kennedy safely into his hotel, Mayor Lugar returned to the streets to confront growing black rage.

> Then I headed out for the next few days, on street corners and in church basements. I made televised statements—the stations gave me a whole half hour just to talk to people about this . . . I was just three months into my term, and I found that I was going to spend a whole year, essentially, in reconciliation, of trying to pull the fabric of the community together.[5]

Race riots did not come to Indianapolis, as they did to Baltimore and other cities that long, hot summer. Even as Mayor Lugar reached out to the black community, he was developing a plan with the help of a citizens' task force that would become his chief legacy to the city. They proposed the consolidation of the city government of Indianapolis with the government of Marion County to create a single entity that soon was called "Unigov." The city limits of Indianapolis were extended to the county boundaries. Like the seven members of the school board, all nine Indianapolis council members had been elected at large, helping assure elite continuity in office. The new council was established with four at-large members and twenty-five elected from districts, assuring minority neighborhoods their own representation. Functions that had been divided between the county and the various municipalities were centralized under the administrative control of the mayor.[6] Under Indiana law, this change could be implemented by state legislative action, without a voter referendum. Lugar lobbied hard, and the legislature approved.

Unigov took effect with dramatic results. The area of Indianapolis increased from 84 to 388 square miles; the 1960 population of 476,258 leaped to 744,624. Suddenly Indianapolis was the nation's eleventh largest city.

When Lugar ran for a second term in 1971, Unigov was the only issue. He won by a landslide. The electorate had been expanded to include all of Marion County, including the suburban Republicans. Indianapolis had been drifting into the familiar pattern of the increasingly black and decaying central city surrounded by the doughnut-shaped white suburbs, with the suburbanites working and relaxing in the central city but not supporting it with taxes or commitment. The economic and cultural unit was Marion County; Unigov made it also the political and governmental unit. Individuals who had lived outside the old city became central to the success of the new one. Middle class (and Republican) energies were enlisted in urban causes, reversing the experience of most large American cities.

Seeking national exposure for their champion, the Indiana Republican organization arranged for Lugar to be a keynote speaker at the 1972 Republican National Convention. The *Washington Post* tagged Lugar as "Nixon's favorite mayor" because of his frequent visits to the White House; in fact, he was the only Republican mayor of a major American city. The label became an epithet when the Watergate revelations nullified Nixon's popularity.

The fortunes of Mayor Lugar were tied to those of the local Republican party in a relationship of mutual benefit. Keith Buhlen offered a summary judgment of the man he regarded as a protégé:

> There's no brighter person and no person who does his homework better. And there's probably no one in the United States Senate that has a better grasp of organizational politics and respect for the two-party system than Dick does, because he came through our college, and our college is the best.[7]

But Dick Lugar remained the Methodist lay preacher in politics, a true heir of Max Beerbohm's Oover, the caricature of an early American Rhodes Scholar. Lugar performed well at the podium, with measured phrases and never-failing articulateness, his earnestness leavened by touches of self-deprecating humor, but he was stiff and ill at ease when slapping backs or shaking hands. Buhlen said that Lugar always seemed out of place when he was taken to campaign in bars.

Paul Sarbanes Goes to Annapolis, Then Washington

While Dick Lugar was winning his victories on the Indianapolis school board, Paul Sarbanes was settling in to the practice of corporation law. But his attitudes toward the law were ambivalent. Some days were fascinating; others were pure boredom. And the ambition nurtured in Oxford still tugged at him. Sarbanes knew that their home in Bolton Hill provided an excellent base from which to campaign for the state legislature. Partly for family financial reasons, he hesitated to take the plunge. His wife understood the ambition and gave him a playful boost. Christine recalls, "I told him if he didn't run, I'd drown him. I couldn't see him sitting around and moaning."[8]

Sarbanes launched an independent campaign for the Maryland House of Delegates. Traditionally, a candidate approached the party clubs to seek a place on the slate cards which the clubs distribute to voters approaching the polls on primary day; winning the Democratic primary is the same as winning the general election in Baltimore.

Sarbanes campaigned from door to door along the brick row houses of Bolton Hill. He would work one side of the street while Christine worked the other. Sarbanes was elected to the House of Delegates in 1966 from the second legislative district of Baltimore, one of thirty-four members of the Baltimore City delegation.

When Sarbanes got to Annapolis, he found other young legislators eager to challenge the power of Marvin Mandel's machine. John O'Brien, who met Sarbanes in January 1967, when they both entered the legislature for the first time, described the group with which they became allied.

> We came into Annapolis at a point in time when Marvin Mandel was the Speaker of the House and Spiro Agnew was the governor. Under Marvin Mandel in the House was a fellow who was deputy majority leader whose name was Dale Hess. A number of us had a sense that Dale Hess was not the kind of person who should be representing our interests as the deputy majority leader. As Young Turks in the legislature, we had a sense that we would try to unseat him . . . We discussed this matter for a while and then one night took a secret ballot vote among ourselves as to who among us we would select to represent what we believed would be the better interests. And Mr. Sarbanes was selected as that person. Word of this—the newspapers called it a cabal—leaked out, and Mr. Hess and his friend Marvin Mandel called in all of their political chits, and people arrived in Annapolis who hadn't been here for years to keep their delegates in line on this issue.[9]

Dale Hess was principal owner of the Tidewater Insurance Company, the holding company for several firms enriched by state contracts. In 1975, he would be convicted of bribery, fined $40,000, and sentenced to three years in prison.[10]

Paul Sarbanes saw that Governor Agnew's program reversed social gains made in Maryland since the 1930s. When Agnew's priorities were solidified in a budget, Sarbanes prepared his own alternative budget overnight and prepared a twenty-two-page comparison of the options. Sarbanes reacted as a legislator's legislator, drawing on his technical mastery of legislative detail. John O'Brien said that the incident "indicated to me the depth of this man, his capacity to understand problems."

Sarbanes labeled Agnew's proposals as the "East Coast version of the Ronald Reagan budget"—Reagan was then the governor of California. The contest pitted one Greek-American against another. After Agnew had been elected vice president, Sarbanes told Garry Wills, "Agnew never did anything for the Greek community in Baltimore except leave it at the earliest opportunity." He also pointed out that Agnew's meteoric rise had never required him to seek reelection to an office. "If he would hold still for a minute, we'd nail him. But he's always moving off to something new."[11]

Governor Agnew was selected as Richard Nixon's running mate at the 1968 Republican Convention. It was the Maryland legislature's duty to choose Agnew's successor. The Senate supported its president, William S. James; the more numerous House supported Speaker Mandel. The outcome was predictable; but a few independent members of the House, including Paul Sarbanes, voted against Mandel.

Party organizations tend to support the status quo. Paul Sarbanes won election to the state legislature in 1966 and reelection in 1968 with some help from Democratic clubs, remnant of the once potent party organization. In 1970, against the advice of veteran Democrats, Sarbanes challenged George Fallon of Baltimore's Fourth Congressional District. Fallon had served twenty-four years in Congress; as chairman of the House Public Works Committee, he brought many federal dollars to Baltimore.

Paul and Christine Sarbanes approached the voters of the Fourth District with the same grass-roots, door-to-door campaign they had utilized in Bolton Hill. Sarbanes created a personal following that transcended party lines. He won the primary with 51 percent of the vote; 45 percent went to Fallon and the remainder to a minor candidate. Sarbanes then won the general election with 70 percent.

Upon entering the House of Representatives, Sarbanes won appointment to the Judiciary Committee and became absorbed in its work. Every year, many members of Congress court interest group favor by introducing their pet bills, knowing the proposals will die in committee. Sarbanes disdained this practice, preferring to devote his energy to molding legislation actually under consideration. He was oriented toward results, rather than showmanship. Colleagues recognized him as a "workhorse" who mastered legislative detail and studied each issue on its merits, although he usually decided to vote for the liberal position. The familiar *Congressional Quarterly* indexes measured Congressman Sarbanes' ideology and partisanship. During his three terms, Sarbanes, on average, opposed the conservative coalition on 87 percent of the relevant votes, and scored 88 percent for party unity.

Maryland was redrawing congressional district boundaries as a result of the 1970 census. Court orders stipulated that the growing suburban citizenry and the decline in Baltimore City's population be recognized. Governor Mandel saw his chance to retaliate for Sarbanes' vote against Mandel becoming governor. Paul Sarbanes was placed in the reshaped Third District, represented by another veteran Democrat, sixty-nine-year-old George Garmatz, chairman of the House Committee on Merchant Marine and Fisheries.

Paul and Christine Sarbanes went into the new district, meeting voters at small gatherings and walking the precincts door to door. Incumbent Garmatz viewed the young Sarbanes' energy with dismay. Rather than attempting to match their activities, he withdrew from the race. Sarbanes overpowered three other candidates to win the primary election with 54 percent, then the general election with 70 percent. He claimed Garmatz's seat on the Committee on Merchant Marine and Fisheries to serve the shipyards of Baltimore.

The period of Paul Sarbanes' service in the House encompassed the revolt of Congress against President Richard Nixon's executive branch. Sarbanes was at the center of the events, collectively labeled Watergate, which constituted a watershed in American constitutional history of the late twentieth century. In what can now be seen as a warmup before the main event, Sarbanes helped lead one of four rebellions against Nixon's foreign policy.[12] In 1974, a coup presumably inspired by Athens toppled the government of Cyprus. Turkey invaded the island with the announced purpose of preventing the union of Cyprus and Greece. Turkish forces, armed with American weapons, invaded areas of the island inhabited by ethnic Greeks. Indiana congressman John Brademas, a Greek-American, drafted resolutions demanding an embargo on further military aid to Turkey on the grounds that American weapons had been used illegally. Paul Sarbanes managed the floor debate successfully; the resolutions passed, and the incident awakened a latent Greek-American political consciousness. But Sarbanes knew that this consciousness was based on more than foreign policy. In 1976, raising funds for his U.S. Senate candidacy, Sarbanes spoke at a Greek-American dinner in Astoria, New York. A reporter described the scene.

> The audience's enthusiasm . . . produced one of [Sarbanes'] most warm and moving speeches of the entire campaign.

Partly in Greek, partly in English, he stirred the audience of hot dog vendors and shipping magnates, construction workers and owners of expensive restaurants, even managing to moisten several pairs of eyes when he said the American Constitution "gives each of us— each of us—a chance to succeed in this country."[13]

In another warmup, Sarbanes testified before committees of both the House and the Senate on Nixon's impoundment of appropriated funds. Nixon's announced purpose was to control inflation; but the funds he withheld had been appropriated for programs Nixon disliked. Sarbanes stated that the practice put the relationships of federalism at risk and described the effects of impoundment on government programs in Maryland. Sarbanes argued that the executive has no legitimate power to impound funds unless he successfully vetoes the initial legislation appropriating them.[14] Sarbanes' conviction was widely shared; the result was the Congressional Budget and Impoundment Control Act of 1974, which reformed the process by which Congress considers the budget and established procedures for considering proposed impoundments (now called "rescissions") by the president.

Through impoundment and other practices, Nixon had thrown down the gauntlet: which branch would dominate the government? In the main event, Congress demonstrated its constitutional ability to check the executive. Public opinion supported the House of Representatives in its move toward the impeachment of President Nixon. That support resulted from the unfolding of information in the Senate Judiciary Committee hearings and the careful building of a case for impeachment by the House Judiciary Committee.

Paul Sarbanes was a very junior member of the Judiciary Committee. He approached the question of impeachment with caution and did not announce any conclusion before hearing all the evidence. The judicial temperament exemplified by Judge Soper served Sarbanes well. In his closing argument to the Judiciary Committee, President Nixon's counsel, James D. St. Clair, argued that the charges against Nixon for the attempted misuse of the Internal Revenue Service and the Department of Justice should be dropped, because the agencies refused to cooperate with the president. Congressman Sarbanes defined the flaw in St. Clair's argument.

The distinguishing characteristic of our system of government that distinguishes it from totalitarian systems, is that we do not sacrifice the means for the end, and it is not only the end result that is important, but the process by which we get there. It is the democratic process that guarantees our freedom to participate in decisions that control how power is to be exercised . . . Because the officials in the institution did not bend and do wrong does not absolve those who sought to make them do wrong.[15]

Because of his independence and caution, Sarbanes was asked to sponsor the first article of impeachment. Millions watched on television as the committee debated the "Sarbanes substitute" for two days. At 7:00 P.M. on Saturday, July 27, 1974, the committee solemnly adopted Sarbanes' language labeling the Watergate break-in part of a pattern of illegal behavior conducted with the knowledge of Richard Nixon. When the Judiciary Committee sent its impeachment recommendation to the full House, President Nixon resigned his office.

The voters of Maryland's Third District had been in the television audience when Sarbanes' first article of impeachment was adopted. He had no opponent in the Democratic primary of 1974, and he won the general election that November with 84 percent of the vote. More important for his future than Sarbanes' celebrity status among these particular constituents was the reputation his cautious judicial temperament won in Congress.

The Election of Two Senators

Sarbanes represented a very safe district. He feared no further retributions by Marvin Mandel and could count on moving up the seniority system over the years to a position of considerable power. But the Sarbaneses felt the time had come to seek statewide office. Maryland's junior senator, Republican J. Glen Beall, the son of a former senator, was up for reelection in 1976. Beall defeated liberal Democratic Senator Joseph Tydings in 1970 with the help of under-the-table money from Richard Nixon's political operation. Beall was also aided by the National Rifle Association, which was outraged at Tydings' support of gun control legislation. Beall consistently supported Nixon on the Vietnam War, while opposing economic legislation that Sarbanes felt would benefit Maryland. Sarbanes was eager for battle against a man he felt failed to represent the interests and needs of Maryland's citizens.

Sarbanes was told that Joseph Tydings, also the son of a former senator, had no interest in attempting to recapture the seat. By the time Tydings changed his mind, Sarbanes' primary campaign was well launched.

The primary had to be won without creating ill feelings within the Democratic party that could cripple Sarbanes' effort in the general election. Furthermore, millionaire Tydings' personal fortune was intimidating. Paul Sarbanes sought campaign contributions from organized labor, his fellow Greek-Americans, and wealthy liberal Democrats.

Sarbanes needed to become known statewide, a process that occupied him and his wife in travel outside the Baltimore area for most of two years. They contacted party leaders and union officials throughout the state, and called on small-town editors in western Maryland, winning many endorsements: retail politics. Meeting other Democrats in small gatherings, Sarbanes emphasized his own humble origins, in contrast to Tydings' wealth. The slogan of his campaign was "From the People, For the People."

Issues mattered. Perhaps looking to the general election, Tydings began to call himself a "moderate" and retreated from some of the positions he had taken in the Senate. Sarbanes criticized his opponent for inconsistency and suggested that Tydings had grown out of touch with his constituents. Sarbanes knew that the Democratic primary voters were more liberal than the general electorate.

Both candidates called on the still fresh memories of Watergate. Tydings pictured himself in a series of television ads as the 1970 victim of "dirty tricks" like those utilized during the 1972 presidential campaign by Nixon's "Watergate crowd." Sarbanes launched a $106,000 ad campaign directed mainly to the Washington suburbs, where he had never before campaigned. The first of the ads showed thirty seconds of images of the House Judiciary Committee in action as the announcer declared:

> When Chairman Rodino needed a leader to break the deadlock between Republicans and Democrats he chose Paul Sarbanes. Paul Sarbanes found the answer . . . This time, it won't be up to Peter Rodino to choose Paul Sarbanes. It will be up to you.[16]

When primary day approached, Paul Sarbanes, the reform Democrat, provided Baltimore party clubs with $53,000 in "walk-around money," a time-honored practice recalling the days of machine politics. The funds assured Sarbanes a place at the top of the club slate cards, the printing and delivery of campaign brochures, and limited get-out-the-vote efforts. On May 18, Sarbanes won the Democratic primary against Tydings and six minor candidates with 55 percent of the vote. His victory was attributed to thorough planning, support of the party organization and organized labor, and the ability to raise and spend twice as much as Tydings.[17]

Although Sarbanes joined Tydings in supporting gun control legislation, the gun lobby concentrated its efforts on defeating Tydings, repeating their 1970 effort. Bumper stickers declared, "If Tydings Wins, You Lose." The plan was to defeat Tydings in the primary, then dump Sarbanes in favor of Beall in the general election. This was a striking political misjudgment. It underestimated both Paul Sarbanes and the three-to-one registration advantage of the Democratic party.

Sarbanes' modest origins remained in the forefront of the general election campaign. His thoughtful demeanor on television during the primary had been called hesitant and uncertain, but now he unleashed his scorn against Beall. The candidates engaged in several raucous, finger-pointing television debates, and Sarbanes thrived on the conflict. He won in November with 57 percent of the vote, becoming the first Greek-American elected to the U.S. Senate. He also ended the Maryland tradition of sending social notables to the U.S. Senate while serious politicians battled for the patronage-rich governorship.

The Second Time Is the Charm

In 1974, Mayor Richard Lugar was called by the Republican state convention to run for the U.S. Senate against the incumbent, a recent contender for the Democratic presidential nomination, Birch Bayh. It was a Democratic year, even in Indiana, and Lugar would not have sought the nomination on his own. But he could hardly reject it, if he hoped to retain the party's backing for future contests. Party leaders feared losing their state legislative majority without a strong banner-carrier; they commissioned a poll which showed Lugar much the strongest person to head the ticket.

Although billed as a contest of ideologies, the campaign became more a contest of style. In the only debate Bayh would agree to, Lugar presented the complexities of economic issues, while Bayh simplified them in a vocabulary appropriate for the television audience. Having survived as a liberal Democrat in a conservative state, Bayh was an experienced and supple campaigner. For conservative audiences, he adopted the persona of a Hoosier farm boy. But Lugar did not try to point out that he had probably worked more days weeding soybeans than Bayh ever dreamed of. He told a TV interviewer, "To suddenly put hayseed in my teeth would be the wrong thing for me . . . [I]t would not only be dishonest, but fatal."[18]

Outspending Lugar by a ratio of five to three, Senator Bayh capital-
ized on an Indianapolis police scandal to carry Mayor Lugar's home
county of Marion, with the same boundaries as the city of Indianapolis.
Lugar carried over half the counties of northern Indiana but only eight of
those south of the old National Road. Nonetheless, Bayh was reelected to
the Senate with just 52 percent of the statewide vote. Lugar's campaign
had been credible, and his standing within the party was undiminished.
In a system like that of Maryland, where candidates are essentially self-
nominated, such a defeat would have blighted his political career.

Dick Lugar accepted a visiting faculty appointment at Indiana State
University for 1975–1976 which allowed him time on the campaign circuit. In 1976, Democratic senator Vance Hartke sought election to a
fourth term, unprecedented in Indiana. From a key committee position,
Hartke helped create Amtrak and Conrail, the federally subsidized rail
systems. He received ample contributions from railroad political action
committees. Depicted as the tool of special corporate interests, Hartke
had been reelected by fewer than five thousand votes in 1970.

Convinced that a Democratic state convention would dump Hartke
for a stronger candidate, the Republican legislature restored primary elections as the vehicle for senatorial nominations in both parties, certain
that rank-and-file Democrats would renominate Hartke. Primaries had
been abolished half a century before, to eliminate the partisan influence
of the Ku Klux Klan. By 1974, the Klan was barely a memory, and the
convention system was a target of political reformers.

Dick Lugar's opponent in the Republican primary was Edgar
Whitcomb, Indiana's governor from 1968 to 1972. Lugar and Whitcomb
argued about their respective administrative records but disagreed over
little but the federal revenue sharing plan, which Lugar supported. When
Whitcomb argued that Lugar was the candidate of "the bosses," Lugar replied that he had not talked to his mentor, Keith Buhlen, in more than a
year. The structure of volunteer enthusiasts and regular party workers
Lugar had established in 1974 gave him the primary victory with 65 percent of the vote.

In the general election, Dick Lugar carried Marion County (Indianapolis) and every jurisdiction north of the old National Road except
urban Lake County and Starke County, a pocket of stubborn rural
Democrats. He added twenty-five counties in southern Indiana to the
eight he carried in 1974. While President Gerald R. Ford was carrying Indiana in the presidential contest by 53 percent, Lugar won the Senate seat
by 59 percent.

The Impact of Apprenticeships

Paul Sarbanes came to the Senate with legal training, like a majority of his colleagues, and with prior service in the House of Representatives, like more than a third of his fellow senators. Lugar came with experience as a businessman; in the 102nd Congress, only fourteen senators listed their primary occupation as business. More important, as mayor of Indianapolis, his prior political experience had been as an elected executive. Twenty-six of his colleagues in the 102nd Congress had served as mayor, or governor, or other high state executive position.

The contemporary Senate fits Woodrow Wilson's long-ago description as "the most perfect product of our politics, whatever that politics may be." But how did the specific apprenticeships of Sarbanes and Lugar influence their different senatorial styles? Four differences should be noted. The first is the difference in their basic attitudes toward the role of the federal government and the relationship of its branches. Second is their differing ambitions for office beyond the Senate; third is their different modes of relating to their constituents. These three are intimately related to the fourth difference, which is the contrasting nature of the party organizations and political cultures from which they came.

Paul Sarbanes achieved a local reputation as a leader in the revitalization of the Baltimore Democratic party. Sarbanes' new kind of organization was held together by common views on issues and volunteer work for admired candidates. If the new party organization had leaders, they were candidates and officeholders. The permanent organizational leader (or "boss") has vanished. Paul Sarbanes rather regrets the change.

> I have a lot of respect for the state party structure in which you go around and meet the chairmen of the two parties, and you discover that they are real people of substance in their communities. Maybe I'm seeing history through rosy glasses, but I have the impression that was more the case then than it is now. The people of real substance didn't see party politics as somehow below them, as not something you could get involved in . . . We've been able to draw a lot of good people into participation [to help in my own campaigns].[19]

When asked if this meant that his campaign organization was largely a personal one, Sarbanes replied, "That's pretty much the case these days, I think, for virtually everybody."

This independence meant that Sarbanes' political career was very much his own to manage. There was no strong, established organization to support his campaigns while imposing its own ambitions upon his career. His belief in the positive role of the federal government fit very well with the attitudes of the Democratic majority he joined in the House, and later the Senate. His role in the Watergate proceedings made him a champion of the prerogatives of Congress in opposition to those of the executive branch.

His campaigns for the Maryland legislature and for the House of Representatives were based on the retail politics of canvassing door to door and meeting with small groups. He first utilized television as a candidate for the Senate. His earlier legislative positions were based on service to the constituency; with hardly any standing party organization linking the legislator to his constituents, Sarbanes took a personal interest in individual needs. The relatively small area of Maryland, and the accessibility of its most concentrated populations, in the Baltimore area and the Washington suburbs, enabled him to continue the practice of retail politics. Eighty percent of his constituents live within fifty miles of his Senate office. Unlike the legislators Richard Fenno studied, Sarbanes' relationships with the world are not rigidly divided between a "home style" and a style of governing.[20] Sarbanes' mode of relating to his constituents is the position of attentive listener, one who can solve problems.

Sarbanes is famous among his colleagues for patient listening, particularly on investigative committees, and Sarbanes' primary method for influencing the direction of Congress is the persuasion of his colleagues in private surroundings.

Dick Lugar was recruited by the party organization to run for mayor. The organization served as a link between the mayor and the voters, as with the 192 priority projects, and Mayor Lugar soon used television to communicate with the citizens of Indianapolis, as he did after Martin Luther King's assassination: wholesale politics. Lugar's nature made him somewhat awkward in performing the glad-handing chores of retail politics, which he tended to delegate to staff members. As a senator, Lugar could count on his state offices to provide service to individual constituents. When Lugar returns to Indiana, his schedule is filled with informal talks and formal speeches.

The aspect of their parties which most influences the senators' political styles is the contrasting support the parties are able to provide. The Indiana Republicans have been a separate organization with separate leadership that can recruit candidates, endorse them in the primary, and provide them with money and labor in the general election. Between elections, the organization provides young adherents for the senatorial staff and helps organize events when Lugar flies back to Indiana on weekends. It is easy for Lugar to devote himself to wholesale politics, making public speeches and filming television ads, as the best use of his time in the constituency.

By contrast, the Maryland Democratic organization is hard to find between elections. Its leaders are its officeholders. Paul Sarbanes often campaigns with other Democratic candidates in supermarkets, but he bears sole responsibility for financing his campaign; and his campaign costs are less than Lugar's because Sarbanes is able to practice retail politics to a greater extent, avoiding some of the media expenses found in Lugar's campaigns.

As mayor, Dick Lugar was the policy leader of his party. The city council was his legislature, and its Republican majority was an important tool of governance. He appreciated the importance of party responsibility. This experience may account in part for his loyalty to Presidents Reagan and Bush, in contrast to the Watergate experience that taught Paul Sarbanes to be suspicious of the executive branch.

Finally, ambition. Paul Sarbanes came to the Senate as a very junior member of the Democratic majority, outranked in seniority by men who had dominated the chamber for years. His career was in his own keeping. The traditional road to leadership in the Senate was to serve his constituents well, thus assuring reelection, and wait for the accretion of seniority to place him in positions of power.

Dick Lugar was in a different situation. Indiana Republicans were touting him as a potential presidential or vice presidential candidate as early as 1972, when they won him a speaking part in the Republican National Convention. In 1974, his main goal in the campaign against Birch Bayh was to maintain his credibility with the party. The Republican Senate minority he joined in 1976 had few members of seniority or power. When the Republicans captured the majority in 1980, Lugar's four years of seniority would be significant, and he would reach for positions of leadership.

Notes

1. Woodrow Wilson, *Congressional Government* (Boston: Houghton Mifflin, 1913), p. 195. (First published, 1885.)
2. *Brown v. Board of Education of Topeka, Kansas,* 347 U.S. 483 (1954).
3. Interview with Senator Lugar, July 19, 1991.
4. Interview with Keith Buhlen, September 12, 1982.

5. Interview with Senator Lugar, July 19, 1991. The setting of Kennedy's speech, and most of the speech itself, is in Arthur M. Schlesinger, Jr., *Robert Kennedy and His Times* (Boston: Houghton Mifflin Co., 1978), pp. 873–876. The speech is quoted in its entirety in David Halberstam, *The Unfinished Odyssey of Robert Kennedy* (New York: Random House, 1968), pp. 85–86. Recalling the event after twenty-three years, Lugar confused his Greek dramatists. Kennedy quoted Aeschylus, not Euripides.

6. The structure of the unified government of Indianapolis and Marion County was described in a pamphlet, *Your Government: Blueprint for the Future,* published by the Marion County Republican Central Committee, which thoughtfully included biographies of the Republican candidates for the elections of 1971.

7. Interview with Keith Buhlen, September 13, 1982.

8. Interview with Paul and Christine Sarbanes, March 3, 1983.

9. Interview with John F.X. O'Brien, July 6, 1982. After nine years in the legislature and four in the state personnel division, O'Brien was in 1982 the director of legislative liaison on the staff of then Maryland Governor Harry Hughes.

10. George H. Callcott, *Maryland and America, 1940–1980* (Baltimore: Johns Hopkins University Press, 1985), pp. 294, 298.

11. Garry Wills, *Nixon Agonistes* (New York: New American Library, 1970), pp. 262–264.

12. James L. Sundquist, *The Decline and Resurgence of Congress* (Washington: Brookings Institution, 1981), p. 275. Sundquist describes four policies: ending the Vietnam war, linking Soviet trade to Jewish emigration, penalizing Turkey for its Cyprus invasion, and blocking intervention in Angola. He makes the point that these were fairly random negations of executive policy, based not on an overall strategy but on emotions and feelings—and the constituent pressures behind them.

13. Harold J. Logan, "Greeks in N.Y. Contribute for Sarbanes, Brademas," *Washington Post,* October 7, 1976, p. C3.

14. U.S. Senate. 92nd Congress, First Session, "Impoundment of Appropriated Funds by the President, Joint Hearings before the Ad Hoc Subcommittee on Impoundment of Funds of the Senate Committee on Government Operations . . . ," p. 224.

15. U.S. Congress. House of Representatives, 93rd Congress, Second Session. "Debate on Articles of Impeachment, Hearings of the Committee on the Judiciary . . ," pp. 74–75.

16. Bill Peterson, "Sarbanes Begins Television Blitz," *Washington Post,* April 22, 1974, p. B1.

17. Bill McAllister and Harold J. Logan, "Sarbanes Easy Victor," *Washington Post,* May 19, 1974, p. A1.

18. Jules Witcover, "Sen. Bayh's Style Frustrates Underdog Candidate Lugar," *Washington Post,* October 28, 1974, p. A2

19. Interview with Senator Sarbanes, July 5, 1982.

20. Richard F. Fenno, Jr., *Home Style: House Members in Their Districts* (Boston: Little, Brown, 1978).

CHAPTER 6

Partisanship, Ideology, and Choice

Some students of Congress have argued that most of its members' actions can be explained by a single motive, the desire for reelection.[1] In extreme form, this claim reduces legislators to calculating machines, weighing each decision for its electoral consequences. I have argued that the influences upon senatorial choice include not only the external factors of constituency and party but also the internal ones of personality and ideology. The sum of these four determinants produces the policy preference, seen as the fifth influence. The policy choice is then considered in the framework of the political context, which is the sixth influence.

This model of six influences must be applied to two different kinds of choice. The first type is choices required by the progress of the institution, when issues are put to a vote. Unless he is the majority or minority leader, the individual senator cannot control the timing of such a choice. However, an individual senator can delay particular roll-call votes almost indefinately by withholding consent to a unanimous agreement proposed by the party leaders which sets times for debate and voting.

The senator has a varying amount of information about, and interest in, the matters brought to a vote. One vote may represent the culmination of a crusade which the senator has led. Another may be a relatively new issue to the senator, who receives the advice of a staff member and considers his policy preference in the light of the political context while riding the Senate subway to reach the Senate chamber.

But roll-call voting does not consume the majority of a senator's day, and the senator is free to determine how the balance of his time shall be invested. Thus the second type of choice, made at the senator's own initiative. Such a choice may range from deciding which concurrent committee meeting to attend or which telephone call to accept, to selecting issues to investigate and planning strategies for achieving policy goals.

This chapter will examine twenty years of records from the *Congressional Quarterly*'s quantitative analysis of the first type of choice, the roll-call vote. The chapter then will examine certain voluntary choices made by the two senators in their first term of office: choosing their initial committee assignments and launching their first legislative initiatives.

Benchmarks of Partisanship and Ideology

Is there a way to determine the mind-set that the two senators brought to the Capitol in 1977? I happened to interview them in August of that year as part of a different project; they were two of 177 respondents in five American cities.[2] My open-end questions were designed to stimulate reflection. When I asked the two freshman senators to define two or three major issues facing the nation, both interpreted the question broadly. Paul Sarbanes spoke to the basics.

> I think there are three issues or problems that always face the nation that are sort of fundamental. One is the integrity of your government . . . The other is the question of war and peace. And the third is the economic question . . . If you're in pretty good shape on those three issues, you can pretty well address most of the others. These go to whether a person has a job, and is therefore able to support his family. It goes to the question of whether their young sons and daughters are going to go off and perhaps lose their life. And it goes to the question of whether the government, in all of its workings, is honest and open and responsive, and carries out its democratic principles and ideals.

Sarbanes' 1977 statement reflected the searing national experiences of Watergate and Vietnam, questions that he dealt with in the House of Representatives. But the issues he named have permanent relevance.

When I asked Dick Lugar to define the two or three most important issues, his answer came in rounded phrases worthy of Max Beerbohm's Oover, the sincere American Rhodes Scholar of 1911.

One of the most important issues is the age-old issue of how powerful the state ought to be in relationship to individuals and
families . . . People feel over-controlled and they would like less government interference in their lives; but it's also a fact that many people
want more governmental services and see the federal government frequently as a superior provider . . . A second major issue is sort of an
age-old quest for whether freedom of initiative and ambition to succeed or push ahead the wheels of individual invention, progress, are
more important than a quest for equity, and what people perceive as
justice, fairness . . . The third basic issue is . . . whether as a person
you really like the idea of individual responsibility and a theology
that would suggest that this is God-given and the responsibility is to
God, as opposed to both a theology—if it's that—and a secular political philosophy that in essence says, people have got to be manageable and they are almost interchangeable, and it's a question of whether
any are going to live if we don't organize them, keep down their ap-
petites and sort of keep them in line.

While Lugar did not insist on libertarian conclusions, he found the
issues raised by the libertarians of central importance. He preferred regulation by market forces to regulation by government, and he saw a tendency in the Democratic party to curtail individual liberty in furthering
an abstract concept of justice. Toward the end of the interview, I asked
him to define what the Republican party stands for.

The Republican party is perceived, or ought to be perceived, as the
party that, at least relative to the Democratic opposition, stands for
a greater reward for personal initiative, would see risk and
investment . . . as things that ought to be encouraged by public
policy . . . [T]he Republican party is always going to be wrapped up
in this issue of the individual and the relationship to the state, favoring more freedom for the individual.

There was a striking congruence between what Lugar saw as the important (even if "age-old") issues and his conception of Republican
principles. There was no hint that Lugar would favor governmental coercion to achieve conformity in social behavior. Nor, on that occasion,
did he volunteer a discussion of Edmund Burke's vision of society as a
living organism.

I found that Paul Sarbanes' conception of the meaning of the Democratic party was more client-oriented. I asked him what distinguishes the
Democratic party from the opposition.

Oh, I think the Democrats are sort of really more the party of working people. They're the party that has always sought to open up American society. I've been very sensitive to that—you know, to the immigrant groups, the minority groups. They have that vision of opportunity. And the Republicans are more the party of status and wealth.
Now, that's a simplification, but I think there is that difference. It gets
clouded, and remains clouded today because of regional
differences . . . so that a Republican in New York State may . . . appear
to be more sensitive to working interests than a Democrat in some
southern or western state. But, within the context of that state, this
distinction probably applies.

These 1977 statements supply a benchmark for comparing the partisanship and ideologies Sarbanes and Lugar brought to the Senate with at-
titudinal changes after their two decades of service to the institution. As a
traditional liberal, Sarbanes believed in the ability of government to solve,
or at least ameliorate, social and economic problems. As a Democrat, he
saw working people as key constituents. As a Maryland senator, a major
focus of his efforts would be to assure Maryland of its fair share, or more,
of federal programs and funds. Dick Lugar, concerned about governmental threats to liberty, would oppose governmental intervention in most
economic matters and would attack bureaucracies and federal spending.
However, he could happily accept credit for federal dollars sent to Indiana, conceding that some citizens regard the federal government as a superior supplier of services.

Although both were seared by that decade of protest and rebellion,
their political values were formulated before the social upheavals of the
1960s. Lugar's conservatism owed much to Robert A. Taft, although he
rejected Taft's isolationism; Sarbanes' liberalism owed even more to
Franklin D. Roosevelt and Adlai Stevenson. Their heroes were politicians
who could see mutual compromise as a mark of progress.

Unavoidable Choices: The Roll-Call Votes

Senators cast hundreds of votes, making a permanent record, during each
session of Congress. The familiar indexes calculated by *Congressional Quarterly* help assess the individual senator's contribution to the aggregate
decisions of the Senate during a single year, as well as measuring change
over time. Two dimensions of their voting are displayed over twenty years
for Senators Lugar and Sarbanes in Table 6–1 (pp. 88 and 89).

Political scientists and political practitioners often decry the lack of cohesion among parties and hunger for the disciplined and responsible parties found in the British Parliament.[3]

While voters may find it difficult to sort out the actions of individual legislators, they can readily hold parties responsible for governmental outcomes. The party unity voting score measures the contribution of individual members to this responsible party ideal.

Richard Lugar and Paul Sarbanes came to the Senate as dedicated partisans. The party unity index for 1977, their first year in the Senate, shows Lugar ranked first among the Republicans, and Sarbanes first among the Democrats. These freshmen were more partisan in their voting than their most outspoken senior colleagues. If the party position is defined by what 51 percent of its Senate members vote for, Sarbanes was more Democratic than Majority Leader Robert C. Byrd or even the Senate's then deputy president pro tem, Hubert H. Humphrey. Lugar was more Republican even than Minority Leader Howard Baker of Tennessee or the conservative gadfly, Jesse Helms of North Carolina.

The party unity index does not measure any role played by ideology in assuring party cohesion. A second index concerns the ability of a coalition based on ideology rather than party to win in the Senate. The conservative coalition forms on any vote in which a majority of Republicans vote the same as a majority of southern Democrats. In 1977, the same year they led their respective parties in unity voting, Paul Sarbanes ranked second among northern Democrats in opposition to the conservative coalition, while Richard Lugar ranked second among Republicans in support of it. Not only was Sarbanes a partisan Democrat, he was a liberal; not only was Lugar a partisan Republican, he was a conservative.

These data reveal Paul Sarbanes' long-lasting agreement with the Democratic party majority. He ranked first in the party unity index for nine of twenty years and never ranked below fourth. His record in relation to the conservative coalition is nearly as striking. He led voting opposition to the coalition for six years and never ranked below sixth among coalition opponents, except for 1982 and 1992.

The 1982 deviation turns out to have a simple explanation. The index of support shows the percentage of times the individual voted with the conservative coalition; conversely, the index of opposition shows the percentage of times votes were cast against it. However, if the individual misses a particular vote, no adjustment is made. Percentages are still based on the total number of times the conservative coalition formed. In 1982, Paul Sarbanes did not participate in seventeen of the ninety-four

TABLE 6-1

Senators Lugar and Sarbanes: Party Unity and Conservative
Coalition Scores

Year		Party Unity			Cons. Coalition		
		Unity	Oppn.	Rank*	Supp.	Oppn.	Rank†
				CARTER			
1977	Lugar	91%	8%	1	95%	4%	2
	Sarbanes	92	6	1	4	94	2
1978	Lugar	85	14	4	80	20	9
	Sarbanes	94	5	1	6	91	3
1979	Lugar	90	10	5	90	10	7
	Sarbanes	88	10	3	8	91	1
1980	Lugar	80	12	11	85	10	14
	Sarbanes	87	11	2	4	92	1
				REAGAN			
1981	Lugar	93	7	4	90	10	15
	Sarbanes	93	6	1	7	93	1
1982	Lugar	85	14	18	84	16	23
	Sarbanes	91	3	2	2	78	13
1983	Lugar	92	8	2	95	5	5
	Sarbanes	88	9	3	11	84	4
1984	Lugar	94	6	4	87	13	24
	Sarbanes	94	2	1	0	98	1
1985	Lugar	92	8	5	88	12	20
	Sarbanes	90	5	3	8	87	4
1986	Lugar	89	10	11	88	9	23
	Sarbanes	96	3	2	3	95	1
1987	Lugar	77	20	24	78	13	24
	Sarbanes	95	4	1	6	94	1
1988	Lugar	76	19	15	86	14	17
	Sarbanes	96	4	1	8	92	3
				BUSH			
1989	Lugar	83	15	25	84	11	18
	Sarbanes	95	4	3	11	87	6
1990	Lugar	86	12	12	97	3	7
	Sarbanes	93	7	4	11	89	4

(continued)

TABLE 6–1 (continued)

Year		Party Unity			Cons. Coalition		
		Unity	Oppn.	Rank*	Supp.	Oppn.	Rank†
1991	Lugar	88	11	17	83	10	21
	Sarbanes	96	4	1	13	88	3
1992	Lugar	86	12	20	76	21	15
	Sarbanes	96	4	2	11	89	11
				CLINTON			
1993	Lugar	88	12	16	88	10	17
	Sarbanes	98	2	1	12	88	3
1994	Lugar	78	22	18	78	22	43
	Sarbanes	98	2	1	13	88	6
1995	Lugar	88	7	32	79	16	43
	Sarbanes	95	4	2	95	4	5
1996	Lugar	88	10	42	92	8	27
	Sarbanes	94	6	2	18	82	6

* Rank within the senator's own party

† Lugar's rank among Republicans in support of the coalition; Sarbanes' rank among Northern Democrats in opposition to the coalition.

Source: *Congressional Quarterly Annual, 1977–1996*

votes on which the coalition took form. These votes were concentrated on five different days. Although he participated in 91 percent of nearly five hundred roll-call votes that year, absence on those five days lowered his percentage of opposition to the conservative coalition to 78 percent. He voted with the coalition only two times during the year—once on a question concerning the administration of price supports for tobacco, and a second time on the issue of federally mandated busing to achieve school integration. The latter exception demonstrates a rule: even Paul Sarbanes can part company on rare issues with his liberal colleagues.

In contrast to Sarbanes' remarkable constancy, Richard Lugar's scores have changed, and the change seems permanent. He has turned away from voting unity with his Republican colleagues, and his support for the conservative coalition has fallen significantly. In 1982, Lugar faithfully supported the coalition—and President Reagan—on budget issues. He voted against the coalition—and with Paul Sarbanes—on twelve occasions. One vote was on an amendment requiring members of Congress to publish their tax returns in the *Congressional Record*. Several were votes on environmental issues and a series of votes were regional in nature, as Lugar joined colleagues from the East and Midwest in an unsuccessful effort to force the corporate farmers of the West to pay a share in the costs of federal irrigation projects.

Lugar's support for the conservative coalition has never come near his top ranking of 1977. His rank among supporters of the coalition fell to twenty-three in 1982 and remained in the high teens or low twenties through 1993, but plunged with the coming of Newt Gingrich's Republican revolution. Similarly, Senator Lugar's top rank in party unity for 1977 has never been repeated. In 1980 he sank to number eleven in the party unity rankings and to number eighteen in 1982. His party unity score returned to former levels for the next three years but then resumed its plunge. In 1987 and 1989, his party unity score was in the lower half of the Senate Republicans; in 1995 and 1996, it was in the lower quarter. The numbers are misleading. Dick Lugar's convictions have remained relatively constant, while some Republican senators elected long after Lugar would write into law certain convictions that Lugar does not share.

Voluntary Decisions: The First Committee Assignments

When they entered the Senate, the first concern of both Sarbanes and Lugar was to negotiate the best possible committee assignments. When I interviewed Sarbanes in August 1977, I asked him to name his priority issues in the Senate.

> First of all, they relate closely to Maryland concerns. There's a tendency, given the way Congress works, to relate your issues and interests to the committees on which you serve, because that puts you into an early role in the decision-making process. I'm on the Banking, Housing, and Urban Affairs Committees, and I've been very much into the anti-boycott legislation issue ... And I'm on the Foreign Relations Committee. So you have a whole range of involvements.[4]

Some senators, including J. William Fulbright of Arkansas, have seen membership on the Foreign Relations Committee as an opportunity to wield policy influence without constraint by interests in their states, because the public pays little attention to foreign affairs, at least in peacetime. But Sarbanes believes that Maryland is more sophisticated than other states concerning international matters because of first-rate news-papers in Baltimore and the District of Columbia, plus the national media centered in Washington. With a major seaport in Baltimore, the state has a long tradition of involvement in international commerce. So Sarbanes felt that he would be representing Maryland concerns on the Foreign Relations Committee, just as he had done on the House Committee on Merchant Marine and Fisheries.

The clear role for Paul Sarbanes, as one of sixty-two Democrats, was to earn respect for his legislative competence, but not contend with his senior colleagues for the spotlight; as he grew in seniority, he would grow in influence. In the meantime, he could accomplish much if he did not insist on taking credit for his accomplishments. Such a role was perfectly in keeping with Sarbanes' personality. In the Maryland legislature and the House of Representatives he developed the habits of a legislator's legislator who wins the respect of colleagues through caution, hard work, and dependability, but does not compete with them for public acclaim.

Coming to the Senate from two terms as mayor of Indianapolis, Dick Lugar was less likely to keep a low profile. Freshman senators are no longer expected to serve a silent apprenticeship. On his first day, Lugar took sides in the contested election of a Senate minority leader on behalf of Howard Baker, who had visited Indianapolis when Lugar was mayor. Baker won by a single vote; Lugar found a particularly grateful mentor. Baker showed his gratitude by naming former naval intelligence officer Lugar to the Select Committee on Intelligence.

Dick Lugar saw himself in the vanguard of a national movement toward conservatism and the Republican party. He frequently cited the June 1978 victory of Proposition 13, California's property tax-cutting initiative, as evidence of a national mood opposing the cost of big government. He wrote stern essays in support of the balanced budget amendment for the op-ed page of the *Washington Post*.[5]

Lugar realized that his status as one of only thirty-eight Republicans provided extra opportunities for involvement, because there were fewer senators to meet all the party's responsibilities, and he saw his opportunities as connected with his committee assignments. In the summer of 1977, I asked him about his committees.

> My committee assignments are Agriculture, Forestry, and Nutrition; Banking, Housing, and Urban Affairs; and the Select Committee on Intelligence . . . I chose them for fairly obvious reasons, in terms of serving Indiana. The Agriculture, and the BHU Affairs hit both ur-

ban and rural people, in their economic interests and lifestyles . . . In the Agriculture Committee, I can contribute not only in a parochial way, to help Indiana farmers, but in a national sense, as the food issue clearly cross-cuts international relationships. The Intelligence Committee . . . offers a good window . . . on what the prospects of war and peace are likely to be.[6]

While Sarbanes described his committee assignments primarily in terms of opportunities to serve Maryland, one sensed Lugar's ambition to make an impact beyond Indiana. He saw implications for international affairs in the work of the Agriculture Committee, which some senators would see only as a place at the pork barrel. Lugar's eagerness to return to the international issues he had dealt with under Admiral Burke's tutelage was transparent. Two years later, when a vacancy occurred on the Foreign Relations Committee, Lugar sought and won it.

Senator Sarbanes, former assistant to Chairman Heller of John Kennedy's Council of Economic Advisers, soon joined the Joint Economic Committee, which, as its name implies, has members from both the Senate and the House. It is a fact-finding committee which issues reports on economic conditions but, like other joint committees, does not recommend specific legislation.

First Legislative Initiatives

Senators do far more than participate in roll-call votes. In committee meetings and floor debates, as well as public forums, effective senators set the agenda and formulate the questions that roll-call votes decide. Richard Fenno suggests that freshman senators need to see an issue all the way from committee decision through floor action before their adjustment to the Senate is complete.[7] Both Dick Lugar and Paul Sarbanes quickly achieved this milestone. Thousands of causes compete for a senator's attention. The ones Sarbanes and Lugar chose for initial activity implemented the policy preferences they expressed to me in August 1977.

Dick Lugar found a cause close to his heart in the work of the Banking, Housing, and Urban Affairs Committee (BHUA). This was assuring the "sunset"—abolition of an outmoded bureau and the policy it administers—of the Renegotiation Board, which was established as a temporary agency in 1952 at the height of the Korean War effort to monitor small defense contractors to be sure they did not make an unreasonable profit.

The Renegotiation Board developed a complex system of reports; when it attempted to recover "excess" profits, courts reversed the board's findings in about half the cases.

Congress routinely reauthorized the existence of the board for twenty-four years. In 1976, the board was told to resolve its backload of cases without taking on any new ones. However, in 1977 bills were introduced to renew the board's existence. Dick Lugar participated in the committee hearings. He argued that, although the agency recovered more than its cost of operation, the costs to industry of complying with the board's requirements (estimated at $100 to $200 million) were passed on to the taxpayer in higher contract costs; and the high costs of compliance discouraged small firms from even bidding on defense contracts. Also the board had never defined what constitutes an "excess" profit.

The two bills were reported to the Senate calendar but were never scheduled for a vote; the leadership felt other issues were more pressing. Lugar continued to insert items into the *Congressional Record* demanding the demise of the Renegotiation Board. In April 1978, the board claimed jurisdiction over contracts to produce weapons for foreign nations and claimed that its staff and appropriations should be tripled to discharge this new responsibility. In May, Lugar testified before the House Appropriations Committee, labeling the Renegotiation Board "a superfluous and counterproductive bureaucracy." The appropriation provided funds for closing down the agency. Last-ditch efforts were made to revive the board in April 1979. Lugar led the floor fight against the relevant amendment, which was defeated, 28–56. The Renegotiation Board could at last rest in peace.

Meanwhile, Dick Lugar became involved in a BHUA issue that received much more public attention. This was the renewal of federal efforts to stave off the bankruptcy of New York City. In February 1978, the Carter administration proposed renewal of the loan guarantee program that had been instituted in 1975. The proposal met a stone wall of bipartisan opposition in the BHUA Committee. On March 16, Lugar declared on the Senate floor, "It will be no service to New York City or to any other city to paper over the cracks once again."[8]

Because both BHUA chairman William Proxmire and ranking minority member Jake Garn were opposed to any relief for New York, freshman senator Lugar could become involved without invading his seniors' interests. He began to draft amendments to the House bill that would meet conservative objections. If legislation were to be passed, he wanted it to be "responsible" legislation. He introduced the amended version to the Senate on June 14, stating that his objects were to limit the exposure of the federal taxpayer by reducing the amount guaranteed, tighten congressional supervision, induce New York to balance its budget quickly, and incorporate safeguards against other cities and states seeking similar support. Lugar's bill was referred to BHUA, which reported it favorably on June 16 by a vote of 12–3. Paul Sarbanes joined the bill's supporters. Minority Leader Howard Baker announced his support of the legislation on June 29, and it passed the Senate that day by a vote of 53–27. Jimmy Carter signed the New York City Loan Guarantee Act of 1978 on August 8.

If the federal treasury could bail municipalities out of financial difficulties, what about private corporations? Congress had already provided loan guarantees to keep the Lockheed aircraft corporation afloat. Following record losses in 1978, the Chrysler Corporation faced bankruptcy. The third largest auto maker employed 200,000 workers; 20,000 were in Indiana. In November, President Carter recommended loan guarantees of up to $1.5 billion and turned the matter over to Congress. In the Senate, this meant the BHUA. Dick Lugar attended all the hearings and took the lead in drafting the legislation, along with Democrat Paul Tsongas, then a senator from Massachusetts.

Lugar outlined his requirements for the legislation: that all parties to the action make their commitments clear; that those parties be prepared to make sacrifices in return for public aid; that there be a mechanism for reviewing the use of the funds; and that the terms be so harsh that applications from other corporations would be deterred.

Senate debate centered on the contribution to be made by labor, represented by the United Automobile Workers. Lugar insisted that labor make a substantial sacrifice to obtain federal help. He began by suggesting a three-year wage freeze valued at $1.32 billion. On December 18, he proposed an $800 million contribution by the hourly workers. The key senators finally agreed on a figure of $525 million from hourly workers and $150 million from nonunion employees. The legislation was accomplished.

In their final forms, both these loan guarantees won wide Senate support, including that of Paul Sarbanes. Lugar changed the legislation, supported by liberals, to suit his conservative colleagues through revisions described in impeccably conservative rhetoric. But why? The failure of Chrysler would have affected a number of his constituents, but Hoosiers have seldom expressed charitable impulses toward New York City. Years later, when a reporter pointed out that free-market conservatives were appalled by both measures, Lugar responded,

> If we had sent Chrysler into bankruptcy and all the people dependent on it had lost their jobs, that would have caused a very considerable crisis of confidence in our economic system. Conservatives just don't do that. That goes even more so for New York City. In a federal system, to chuck all that up in the air would be totally irresponsible.[9]

Thus Lugar's libertarian concern for freedom over regulation was tempered by Edmund Burke's vision of society as a living organism.

Lugar's convictions were also engaged in the work of the Committee on Agriculture. At issue was the question of amending the Federal Insecticide, Fungicide, and Rodenticide Act (FIFRA). Assigned the duty of determining the safety of some thirty-five thousand chemical pesticides, the Environmental Protection Agency had accumulated a huge backlog of applications for safety certification. Lugar claimed that good government intentions created intolerable delays and costs for the farmer. Since all the products were combinations of some fourteen hundred chemicals developed and produced by four or five large corporations, the proposed legislation seemed reasonable. It directed the EPA to concentrate on the fourteen hundred chemical ingredients, rather than the thirty-five thousand combinations. The revised FIFRA was signed by Jimmy Carter on September 30, 1978.

While Dick Lugar's initial legislative efforts were devoted either to championing conservative causes, or to making specific governmental activities palatable to conservatives, Paul Sarbanes' first legislative initiative centered on serving Maryland. His first achievement was to guide through the Foreign Relations committee, and then the full Senate, the first change since 1790 in American provisions for the immunity of foreign diplomats from prosecution. Diplomats and their staff members involved in automobile accidents were persuaded by their insurance companies to invoke diplomatic immunity, leaving the accident victims without compensation and the insurance companies enriched by their already collected premiums. The victims were usually citizens of Maryland, the District of Columbia, or New York, where consular offices are concentrated.

Sarbanes presided over one-day Foreign Relations Committee hearings on May 24, 1978. A representative of the insurance industry objected to the stipulation that diplomatic officials be required to carry liability insurance when operating vehicles, vessels, or aircraft, and that injured citizens be enabled to proceed directly against the insurance companies although their clients might be protected by diplomatic immunity. Sarbanes mildly

asked if the insurance companies had ever refused to issue policies to diplomats on the grounds that claims could be avoided through the invoca-
tion of diplomatic immunity. The lobbyist retired into silence.

Sarbanes then presented amendments to the House bill to a meeting
of the full Foreign Relations Committee. The changes were adopted by
voice vote without change and reported favorably. Sarbanes introduced
the legislation for Senate debate on August 17; four senators spoke in favor of the bill; the Senate passed the law by voice vote. The House of Representatives concurred in the Senate changes on September 18, and President Jimmy Carter signed the Diplomatic Relations Act of 1978 on
September 30.

The result would clearly benefit those few Marylanders injured in accidents by foreign diplomats, but the new law was not one to make head-
lines. Paul Sarbanes demonstrated his mastery of the details of the issue,
his understanding of the legislative process, and his willingness to take on
the rather thankless housekeeping tasks that are part of modern legislation. It was a good first bill for a freshman senator beginning to climb the
seniority ladder of the majority party.

Meanwhile, Sarbanes' membership on the Foreign Relations Committee provided him a very public role in debating ratification of the two
treaties with Panama concerning the Panama Canal. Reflecting raging
public controversy, the Senate provided the most detailed examination of
a treaty since the Treaty of Versailles ended World War I and established
the League of Nations. Perhaps mindful of the Senate's rejection of that
treaty, Jimmy Carter claimed that the authority of the presidential office
itself was at stake in the debate.[10]

Sarbanes was in no hurry to announce, or even formulate, his position. Only at the close of committee hearings did Sarbanes announce his
decision and explain his reasons for supporting the treaties. He felt that
some change in the relationship between Panama and the United States
was inevitable, for the colonial era was dead. The treaties offered the opportunity for a controlled improvement of that relationship.

Senator Frank Church of Idaho and Sarbanes as chairman of the
relevant subcommittee were designated as floor leaders of the debate.
The only hope of ratification lay in allowing individual senators to
claim credit for changing the treaties to make them more acceptable.
However, changes of real substance would have to be submitted to
Panama for approval. Amendments are adopted by simple majority
vote, although final ratification requires a two-thirds vote. Needing
only a majority, the opponents submitted "killer" amendments in-

tended to force the treaties' rejection. Sarbanes had to decide which amendments to accept, debate the unacceptable proposals, and then move that the latter be tabled.

While the treaties were under consideration, Sarbanes spoke four or five times on the average day. He responded to points about the effects of the treaties, diplomatic terms, relevant points of international law, and the history of the Canal. Sarbanes was always mindful that, if the treaties were rejected, the United States would have to protect its position in Panama with the use of force.

The two-thirds vote needed for ratification was acquired, with but a one-vote margin. Dick Lugar voted against the treaties. Whenever he appeared in Indiana, members of the audience demanded to know his position on the treaties before allowing him to speak.

A predictable legislative disagreement between Sarbanes and Lugar occurred with the proposed Labor Law Reform Act of 1978. The bill had real teeth and was the top priority of organized labor. Its purpose was to revive union strength by easing the task of organizing workers and winning union contracts.

Business interests lobbied determinedly against the bill's passage in the Senate, calling on the Republican leadership for help. Minority leader Howard Baker asked Lugar and Orrin Hatch of Utah, a freshman member of the Labor Committee, to organize the opposition. They became the floor leaders of a growing filibuster conducted by three teams, each of five or six senators, who took turns holding the floor; they issued a daily bulletin on the progress and prospects of the enlarging filibuster; and they let it be known that, if cloture were invoked, they had readied some twelve hundred amendments which would require consideration. Debate began on May 16, 1978, and continued until June 22.

Dick Lugar's position was that "true" labor reform was indeed necessary, but that this bill was designed to serve special interests. He justified obstructing the Senate's business on populist grounds, arguing that the majority opinion of the American people was being ignored by the Senate. He again cited California's Proposition 13 and mentioned the closing of public schools to save money in Cleveland and Dayton.

The Senate never produced the 60 votes needed to end debate on the Labor Law Reform Act. Six attempts were made to invoke cloture, a new record for the largest number of cloture votes on a single bill. The largest number in favor of ending debate was 58 of the needed 60 on June 13 and 15. On June 22, before the bill was recommitted, only fifty-three senators supported the cloture motion. Paul Sarbanes supported cloture on all six

occasions and co-sponsored the first three cloture petitions. In supporting the bill on the Senate floor, he complained that the filibusterers—he
did not name names—failed to address the substance of the bill. "This
legislation," he declared, "has been put in the posture of embracing concepts which are not contained in it."

With the beginning of a new Congress in 1979, subcommittee assignments were reshuffled. Paul Sarbanes became chairman of the Subcommittee on Securities of the Banking, Housing, and Urban Affairs Committee (BHUA). Its three members were Sarbanes, Democrat Harrison
Williams of New Jersey, and Republican Dick Lugar. The subcommittee
serves as the oversight group in the Senate concerned with the Securities
and Exchange Commission (SEC), an agency established in New Deal
times to police the stock market and associated financial institutions. The
subcommittee's concern was to modernize laws governing the relations
between the SEC and smaller businesses. Inflation had changed the quantitative definition of "small business," but the law had not changed; laws
written for the regulation of giant corporations placed an unnecessary
burden on small firms.

On March 21, 1980, Sarbanes introduced a bill amending the statutes
which govern the SEC. The Securities Subcommittee held hearings on
March 24 over which Sarbanes presided. On July 29, Sarbanes was joined
by eight of the fifteen members of the full BHUA (including Dick Lugar)
in introducing the Small Business Investment Incentive Act of 1980. It
permitted businesses to sell up to $5 million in securities to institutions
and sophisticated investors without meeting the registration and reporting requirements of the SEC, which were designed to protect unwary investors against fraud in the marketplace. This reduced the cost of market-
ing new stock issues from $200,000 to $40,000 for small firms. The
amended bill was passed by the Senate; the House concurred in the Senate amendments; and the bill was signed by Jimmy Carter.

While not directly related to Sarbanes' conviction that the Democrats
are the working man's party, the bill eased the burden of regulation upon
a sector of small business, thus winning the support of Dick Lugar, and
contributed marginally to the employment of the nation's work force.
The ease with which Lugar and Sarbanes switched from opposition on
one bill to cooperation on another was typical of the Senate when it is
working well. Partisan rhetoric need not make enemies; senators of very
different backgrounds and convictions can work together.

Paul Sarbanes and Dick Lugar came to the Senate with different experiences and different expectations. Sarbanes brought his experience in the

Maryland legislature and the House of Representatives. His initial Senate accomplishments demonstrated legislative craftmanship but revealed no desire for public attention. He showed himself a supporter of the working class, voted nearly always with his party's majority, and showed little interest in building bridges to the opposition party, but played an important role in winning ratification of the Panama Canal treaties.

Lugar's executive experience at the storm center of Indianapolis politics probably led him to expect more public attention. He joined the Senate minority, expecting opportunities not available to freshman senators in prior eras because of the shortage of Republican senators to fill the available positions. He was also confident that the national trend was toward conservatism. He helped close down the Renegotiation Board; he signed on to the cause of a balanced budget amendment; he helped simplify the process of pesticide regulation, and he organized an antilabor filibuster. But he did not always emphasize the negative. He realized that, to actually achieve legislation, the minority party must win support from the majority party. And his conservatism was thoughtful. He did not offer knee-jerk opposition to federal programs. He helped make the federal bailouts of New York City and the Chrysler Corporation palatable for conservatives.

Their early roll-call votes demonstrated the depth of disagreement between Lugar and Sarbanes, revealing them as both extreme partisans and convinced ideologues. They negotiated committee assignments which would serve the interests of their states. The legislative initiatives— the causes to which they gave time and energy—were chosen on the basis of their expressed political values. What surprises is the frequency with which each supported the other's legislation. Paul Sarbanes supported Dick Lugar's versions of the financial bailouts for New York City and the Chrysler Corporation. Dick Lugar suported Paul Sarbanes' modernization of the laws governing the Securities and Exchange Commission. They exhibited bedrock disagreement on two major issues, one domestic and one foreign: reform of the labor laws and the Panama Canal treaties.

Their actions showed that both Sarbanes and Lugar were interested in political accommodation. With the possible exception of Lugar's antilabor filibuster, neither sought the kind of disagreement that can end in stalemate.

Notes

1. The clearest statement of this argument is probably David R. Mayhew, *Congress: The Electoral Connection* (New Haven: Yale University Press, 1974).

2. The results were published in *The Guardians: Leadership Values and the American Tradition* (New York: W.W. Norton, 1982).

3. Woodrow Wilson was the intellectual father of this conviction. See his *Congressional Government,* first published in 1885. The most forceful call for responsible parties by political scientists was "Toward a More Responsible Two-Party System: A Report of the Committee on Political Parties," 44 *American Political Science Review,* Supplement (September 1950). The yearning for parliamentary government of a frustrated member of Jimmy Carter's presidential staff was expressed by Lloyd N. Cutler in "To Form a Government," 59 *Foreign Affairs* (Fall 1980), 126–144.

4. Interview with Senator Sarbanes, August 1977.

5. Richard G. Lugar, "The Push for a Balance-the-Budget Amendment," *Washington Post,* January 20, 1979, p. A23, and "The Amendment Is *Not* a Fake," March 26, 1981, p. A17.

6. Interview with Senator Lugar, August 25, 1977.

7. Richard F. Fenno, Jr., *Learning to Legislate: The Senate Education of Arlen Specter* (Washington, D.C.: Congressional Quarterly Press, 1991), p. 85.

8. All quotations of statements on the floor of the Senate are from the *Congressional Record* for the appropriate date.

9. Quoted in George Lardner, Jr., "Lugar Can Cross Allies, Charm Foes, and Outdo Roger Staubach," *Washington Post,* April 27, 1982, p. A2.

10. The story of the Panama Canal treaties has been recounted many times. For the historical background, see David McCullough, *The Path Between the Seas* (New York: Simon and Schuster, 1976). A good brief account of the contest in the Senate is Cecil V. Crabb, Jr. and Pat M. Holt, *Invitation to Struggle: Congress, the President and Foreign Policy* (Washington, D.C.: Congressional Quarterly Press, 1984), pp. 81–92.

CHAPTER **7**

Changing Political Contexts
Policy and Presidential Influence

In the model of senatorial decision making, the political context is the total situation or environment in which the need for choice arises. One of the more obvious aspects of the political context is the identity and party membership of the president, particularly when the chief executive has taken a public position on the choice to be made.

The initial years of Paul Sarbanes' and Dick Lugar's service in the Senate came as Congress was reasserting its constitutional prerogatives in response to the excesses of Presidents Lyndon Johnson and Richard Nixon. The Senate became more assertive as an institution, and individual senators reached for new authority. The result was the fragmentation of power in the Senate. Presidents could no longer create a governing coalition across the barriers of the Constitution by dealing with a few Senate leaders.[1] Gerald Ford inherited a weakened presidency. His modest legislative program met stern resistance, and he lost the bid for reelection in his own right to Jimmy Carter.

Lugar and Sarbanes arrived in Washington as Carter entered the White House. Carter's legislative program offered remedies for a long list of national ills, but he seemed unable to set priorities. All his proposals were equally urgent; while they may have been intellectually separate, Carter could not see that they were politically connected, and his only hope for legislative accomplishment lay in constructing a political coalition in Congress around key issues.

Because the Constitution separates the two branches, a central ingredient of American politics in any era is the magnitude of congressional support which the president is able to win for his policies. *Congressional Quarterly*'s index of presidential support tells the percentage of support or opposition by individual legislators to measures which brought forth a public statement by the president. Loyalty to a president of one's own party and opposition to a president of the other party is not unusual, but it is far from automatic. Table 7–1 displays the presidential support scores of Senators Sarbanes and Lugar for twenty years.

These data suggest the shortfall in Democratic support for President Carter. During Carter's term of office, Paul Sarbanes opposed the president's recommendations from 12 to 25 percent of the time for a particular year. Yet, for all four years, Sarbanes ranked eighth or above among Democratic senators in presidential support. Recalling Carter's administration in 1992, Paul Sarbanes offered a rueful admission that his own party must share the blame for Carter's failures.

> I think that the Democrats, looking back on it now, would probably work harder to cooperate with the president of our own party. We haven't had one for so long that it would behoove us to do that.[2]

This seemed an admission that Democrats were slow to recognize growing public frustration with legislative stalemate coupled with declining support for Congress and its Democratic majority. The Republican resurgence of 1980 may have been a rude surprise to many Democrats, but their partisanship was revived quickly.

Republicans correctly perceived 1980 as a year of opportunity. Half a dozen party leaders contended for the presidential nomination. An early entrant was Senate minority leader Howard Baker, who asked Dick Lugar to serve as his campaign chairman. Baker's Senate duties precluded intense campaigning, and he had taken many positions on the liberal side of the Republican spectrum which made him suspect to the conservative Republican primary electorate. He withdrew from the campaign on March 5.

When the Republican choice was narrowed to Reagan or Bush, and Reagan's lead was growing, the Reagan campaign began to consider publicly the choice of a running mate. Keith Buhlen, Dick Lugar's mentor in Indiana politics, was then working in the Reagan campaign. He recommended the inclusion of Lugar's name in the list of possible running mates.[3]

The Reagan campaign asked freshman senator Lugar for ten years of income tax returns and dispatched Reagan aides to several interviews with him. Appearing on CBS's *Face the Nation* in mid-June, Lugar said he

TABLE 7-1

Senators Lugar and Sarbanes: Presidential Support Scores

Year		Support	Opposition	Rank*
		CARTER		
1977	Lugar	48%	51%	6
	Sarbanes	82	17	5
1978	Lugar	35	64	8
	Sarbanes	87	12	2
1979	Lugar	43	57	14
	Sarbanes	85	12	5
1980	Lugar	44	53	13
	Sarbanes	73	25	8
		REAGAN		
1981	Lugar	90	9	2
	Sarbanes	38	61	3
1982	Lugar	83	15	7
	Sarbanes	25	65	7
1983	Lugar	95	5	1
	Sarbanes	41	58	11
1984	Lugar	92	8	1
	Sarbanes	30	64	6
1985	Lugar	89	10	3
	Sarbanes	22	74	5
1986	Lugar	88	11	13
	Sarbanes	18	81	2
1987	Lugar	76	21	4
	Sarbanes	31	67	3
1988	Lugar	86	13	1
	Sarbanes	40	59	1
		BUSH		
1989	Lugar	93	2	4
	Sarbanes	45	53	10
1990	Lugar	86	11	2
	Sarbanes	31	69	13
1991	Lugar	93	7	3
	Sarbanes	30	70	5

(continued on next page)

TABLE 7-1 (*continued*)

Year		Support	Opposition	Rank*
1992	Lugar	87	10	2
	Sarbanes	27	73	13
			CLINTON	
1993	Lugar	30	65	31†
	Sarbanes	96	4	3
1994	Lugar	45	55	23
	Sarbanes	95	5	4
1995	Lugar	26	67	21
	Sarbanes	90	10	3
1996	Lugar	31	68	13
	Sarbanes	90	10	4

* Displays rank within senator's party in support, when the president is of the same party; rank within the senator's party in opposition, when the president is of the opposing party.

† In 1993, Lugar ranked 31st among Republicans in opposition to President Clinton. Not shown in this table is that he ranked 12th among Republicans supporting Clinton.

Source: *Congressional Quarterly Annual, 1977–1996*

would accept the position if offered, but he endorsed Howard Baker as the best choice Reagan could make.[4] Lugar remained in the spotlight for nearly four months of national publicity. The Lugars were met by a crowd of reporters and cameras when they arrived for the July Republican National Convention. Shortly afterward, Reagan announced his selection of George Bush. In August, Dick Lugar told me with wry satisfaction that the amount of attention paid to his public pronouncements had increased significantly.[5]

Ronald Reagan's genial personality came through strongly in his television debates. Voters agreed with Reagan's picture of a lagging economy, and their votes represented as clear a mandate as an American election can offer to do something about it. Reagan won forty-four states with 50.7 percent of the national vote to 41 percent for Carter and 6.7 percent for Independent John Anderson. The Republican party gained twelve Senate seats to capture an unanticipated majority of three: fifty-three Republicans to forty-seven Democrats. It was the most dramatic change in Senate membership since the Democrats won thirteen new seats in 1958.

Republican membership increased in the House of Representatives by thirty-three seats, but Democrats retained a partisan majority. The Republican minority provided a loyal core, augmented by the "boll weevils," a group of conservative southern Democrats, mostly from districts Reagan carried. Compared to Jimmy Carter, Ronald Reagan's message was more coherent and his staff was prepared to "hit the ground running." A working majority for Reagan's economic program was quickly formulated. Soon to be labeled the Reagan Revolution, the program included tax cuts to stimulate economic growth, monetary policy to curb inflation, domestic spending cuts to balance the budget and reduce the size of government, and a massive defense build-up. George Bush had labeled the program "voodoo economics" during the presidential primary contest.

Senate Republicans knew that their majority status owed much to Reagan. Majority Leader Howard Baker concentrated on maintaining the support of every one of his Republicans; any Democrats who joined would be a bonus. The Senate Republicans were disposed to cooperate, believing that the party must demonstrate its capacity to govern. Their slender majority concentrated Republican attention on the need for unity. Both in committees and on the floor, outcomes merely ratified the decisions of Republican caucuses, frustrating Democrats like Paul Sarbanes accustomed to a majority party that accommodated a wide variety of viewpoints and even permitted interplay with the opposition.

Dick Lugar's support for Republican presidents Reagan and Bush was unwavering. He led Republicans in support of President Reagan three times and ranked below fourth only in 1982, when Reagan vetoed Lugar's economic stimulus bill, and 1986. In 1988, the final year of Ronald Reagan's presidency, Richard Lugar led the Senate Republican party in support for Reagan, with a presidential support score of 86 and an opposition score of 13. Paul Sarbanes, with a support score of 40 and an opposition score of 59, led the Senate Democrats in opposition to President Reagan. In the announcement of these results, pictures of Lugar and Sarbanes look out from opposite pages of the 1988 *Congressional Quarterly Almanac*. Symbolically, they do not glance at each other.

The Birth of Budgetary Stalemate

Dramatic change in the political context was demonstrated by President Reagan's legislative successes. Reagan's budget director, former congressman David Stockman, decided to seek budget cuts first, so tax cuts could be made without seeming to threaten larger budget deficits.[6] In March of

1981, the Senate approved a package that cut $36 billion from the budget after defeating some thirty liberalizing amendments, most of them supported by Paul Sarbanes. The cuts were largely reductions in programs established by Lyndon Johnson's Great Society, such as child nutrition and subsidies for mass transit. But Stockman made concessions to ensure keeping leading Republicans on board. He preserved the tobacco subsidies dear to the heart of Jesse Helms of North Carolina and Tennessee's Clinch River Breeder Reactor, Howard Baker's pet project. He failed to anticipate that other legislators would soon demand the preservation of their own favorite programs. Stockman learned too late that "sacred cows run in herds."[7]

In the House of Representatives, enough Democrats joined the solid Republicans to adopt the administration package by a six-vote margin. The cuts were adopted simultaneously, so it was hard for program beneficiaries to identify individual legislators with the reductions in specific programs and blame them for their votes. Instead, members of Congress were clearly voting for the president's economic program; if it were to be rejected and economic conditions worsened, they could be blamed by their districts' entire electorate.[8]

David Stockman's numbers were based on wildly inaccurate estimates of government revenue, which Stockman later labeled his "rosy scenario." Stockman had to achieve $77 billion in specified cuts, plus an additional $44 billion of cuts yet to be determined, designated merely by a "magic asterisk." This undesignated cut Stockman planned to take from entitlement programs, which are benefits allocated by law to any persons who qualify for them. They include social security benefits, military and civil service pensions, unemployment benefits, and farm subsidies. They made up about half of the federal budget. The ranking Republican and Democrat of the Senate Budget Committee saw entitlement programs as the key to the federal deficit. They offered the administration a bipartisan committee majority in favor of freezing cost-of-living increases in federal entitlements for a full year. This did not fit Stockman's secret plan. Entitlement cuts were to come only after Congress accepted the discipline of cutting their favorite pork barrel projects. Stockman persuaded President Reagan to make an unusual trip to Capitol Hill to meet with Republicans on the Budget Committee. The president said he was determined to stay with his campaign promise of preserving social security benefits. Although the meeting was private, such pledges do not remain secret. The chance to modify entitlement programs during Reagan's honeymoon period was lost.

The administration pressed on with its tax cut proposal. The supply-side theory was emphasized in its title, the Economic Recovery Tax Act. Cutting marginal tax rates should stimulate entrepreneurial energy and investment, creating jobs. True supply-siders argued that the reduced rates would bring such prosperity that government tax revenues would actually increase. The plan was basically the Kemp-Roth proposal for a 30 percent cut in income tax rates implemented over a three-year period, added to a faster method of depreciating business investments. This provision for a tax preference ("loophole" to its opponents) by the administration set off a bidding war among congressmen for their own favorite tax preferences, which Stockman accepted to win votes for the final bill.

On July 27, 1981, President Reagan addressed the nation on television, asking voters to demand that their representatives pass the administration's tax cut bill, rather than the anemic Democratic version. Some legislators knew the popularity of the president in their districts and were not about to oppose him; others were pleased with the inclusion of the tax loopholes favored by strong interest groups. The bill had something for everybody. On July 29, all but eight Senators approved it; the House agreed, 282–95.

Dick Lugar and Paul Sarbanes joined their colleagues in voting for the tax cut. The theory of the bill fit perfectly with Lugar's commitment to the encouragement of private economic initiative; the extent to which the bill would undermine his commitment to a balanced budget was not yet clear. As assistant to Chairman Heller of John Kennedy's Council of Economic Advisers, Paul Sarbanes had been involved with the Kennedy tax cut. The economic expansion which followed increased federal revenues; whether the tax cut caused the expansion is still debated. Historically, tax cuts had been so rare that Sarbanes felt he should support even an imperfect one. He voted for the bill, hoping that acceptable amendments would come at a later day. (Some did, in the tax reform of 1986.)

Thus Lugar and Sarbanes helped create budgetary stalemate. Congress cut back programs with small or local constituencies, like harbor dredging and urban mass transit subsidies, but it dared not touch programs like social security, which have large and vocal constituencies. The result was that the total national debt accumulated by all administrations from George Washington through Jimmy Carter was tripled by the end of Ronald Reagan's second term. Despite devices like the Kemp-Roth and Graham-Rudman legislation and "budget summit" agreements with President Bush, the deficit grew.

Disagreement led to stalemate. If they had controlled all branches of the government, Democrats would have raised taxes on the wealthy. If

Republicans had been in complete charge, they would have cut social programs. Each party could thwart the other's plans but was unable to carry out its own. Congress rejected President Bush's plan for attacking the 1990–1992 recession; Bush then vetoed the program adopted by Congress. Either plan might have been better than nothing.

Long before the magnitude of the deficit problem became clear, Sarbanes and Lugar were dealing with the immediate result of adopting Reagan's financial policies, which was a sharp economic recession. Economic circumstances in 1981 were not the same as those underlying the Kennedy era tax cut. Tight monetary policy, aimed at controlling inflation, had an immediate impact. Credit was restrained while the supply of money contracted. High interest rates devastated industries such as home building that are particularly sensitive to interest charges. Both the tax cut stimulus and the equipment write-off provisions of the new tax law required a business climate favorable to investment, and adequate time, to have an impact. Neither condition prevailed. By November 1982, the American economy declined more sharply than in any similar period since the Great Depression. Nine million Americans were unemployed. Seventeen thousand businesses failed in 1981.

President Reagan claimed that he inherited the situation; decades of "tax and spend" by the Democrats had been a national "binge" that could only be cured by suffering. Thus he told the nation to "stay the course." In time, he felt (correctly), the economy would recover. But the House of Representatives and a third of the Senate (including Dick Lugar and Paul Sarbanes) could not wait. They sought reelection that November.

Senator Lugar's Response to Economic Distress

The economic aspect of the political context was grim. But Dick Lugar's party now held the Senate majority. The early influence on the legislative process which Paul Sarbanes had enjoyed as a subcommittee chairman passed to Lugar.

As the recession deepened, Dick Lugar grew increasingly restive. The situation in Indiana grew worse. Steel production fell to a third of capacity. Residential construction was at a standstill. Automobile plants were all but closed; more than 300,000 Hoosiers would be unemployed by election day. Would Indiana's economic distress have bothered Lugar so much if he had not been a candidate for reelection? His Burkean concern for the fabric of society, displayed earlier in the Chrysler and New York City bailouts, seems an adequate explanation for at least one economic policy disagreement with Ronald Reagan. Lugar found a solution suggested by the representatives of the housing industry, familiar to him as chairman of the Housing and Urban Affairs Subcommittee of the Banking Committee (BHUA).

On March 17, 1982, Lugar introduced a "bill to amend the National Housing Act to provide for emergency interest reduction payments and other purposes." The measure was a highly targeted economic stimulus through immediate aid to the housing industry. In introducing the bill, Lugar said it was designed to achieve three principles:

> First, it must create the greatest amount of jobs in the shortest amount of time. Second, it must be consistent with the overall economic recovery program passed by Congress last year. Last, it must be temporary and not establish a permanent federal financial involvement.[9]

The interest rate on first mortgage loans was then 16 percent. The bill would supply loans reducing that rate as much as 4 percent—a federal subsidy for interest rates to make new homes affordable again. The subsidy would be made available to 300,000 to 450,000 families with less than a $30,000 annual income when they purchased newly constructed or substantially rehabilitated homes. Subsidies would be repaid upon the sale or refinancing of the home, so the Treasury would recapture its investment.

The bill was referred to Lugar's subcommittee, which reported it unanimously, claiming in its report that the initial $1 billion expenditure would immediately produce new jobs and "generate $2.5 billion in additional income taxes," so there would be no additional costs until 1984.[10]

The support for Lugar's proposal was overwhelming. Mortgage brokers, building trades unions, and investment bankers favored the measure. Realtors wanted it to include provisions for the purchase of some used homes. In the committee hearings, twelve organizations representing low income interests argued that it would be unconscionable to provide this assistance for middle-income home buyers without aiding the needy. Lugar held to the purpose of economic stimulus. He would not broaden the bill's target for either paupers or real estate brokers. The media covered the progress of the proposal as the only jobs bill in Congress with a chance of avoiding a presidential veto.

Industry lobbyists deployed among both House and Senate office buildings. The House passed its companion measure on May 11, attaching it to an omnibus supplemental appropriations bill to ensure its immediate consideration. Lugar attempted to follow the House lead by attaching the

Senate bill to the same appropriations bill as a nongermane amendment. Senator William Armstrong of Colorado launched a filibuster designed to block the bill. Lugar and Majority Leader Baker worked out a rare procedural maneuver. Cloture was invoked by a vote of 95–2. Then, instead of appealing the chair's rule that the amendment was nongermane, which would have required a simple majority vote, Lugar asked the Senate to waive the rule of germaneness for this occasion, which required a two-thirds vote. His motion was passed by a vote of 63–27. The housing aid bill was then passed, 69–23. Both votes were formidable demonstrations of Senate support, suggesting that the Senate could easily muster the two-thirds vote necessary to override a Reagan veto.

Paul Sarbanes supported the bill. When asked about it, he replied,

> It was a reflection of the plight of the housing industry and the effective pressures of the home builders and others . . . It ended up being the thing to do. And it became the thing to do because it represented an initiative from the Republican side.[11]

This was a clear description of the changed political context. Dick Lugar and Senator Jake Garn called on the president at the White House, attempting to persuade him to approve the appropriations bill. On June 24, however, the president vetoed the bill, citing the inclusion of the mortgage interest subsidy program as his reason. Reagan wrote to the Congress, "We will not promote a housing recovery by going even deeper in debt. More red ink spending will only make the recession worse."[12]

Either the president did not know about, or was unimpressed by, the "multiplier effect" argument of Keynesian demand-side economics that new jobs would increase tax revenues. In 1992, Dick Lugar told me that President Reagan never understood the housing bill; "Ed Meese had already written the veto message, long before I got there to plead the case."[13] An attempt to override the president's veto failed in the House, making the question moot in the Senate.

Senator Sarbanes Resists the Conservative Advance

Suddenly finding himself in the Senate minority, Paul Sarbanes watched as the Reagan economic revolution proceeded. The recession of 1981–1982 was no surprise; the strong medicine of the Federal Reserve Board's contraction of credit and money resulted in recession and unemployment, just as predicted by orthodox Keynesian economics. It was strong medicine that the Democrats had not been willing to administer: bringing down inflation at the cost of—even temporary—human misery.

Without a legislative leadership role, Sarbanes launched a series of nonlegislative endeavors best described as the rear guard actions of a liberal Democratic senator forced to retreat by the advancing Reagan legions. His actions nearly supply a catalog of nonlegislative influences available to a senator: dissent from the approval of presidential appointments; supervision, or "oversight," of the federal bureaucracy; the staging of fact-finding hearings; lobbying fellow legislators; and public opposition to the trends of administration action.

After President Reagan's inauguration, virtually the first order of business for the Senate Foreign Relations Committee was to consider the nomination of General Alexander Haig to be secretary of state. Haig had been President Richard Nixon's last White House chief of staff and had served him throughout the Watergate crisis. Sarbanes wanted to be sure that Haig's performance in office would not be tainted by the same disdain for constitutional limits that characterized so many of Nixon's staff. In his final statement of the hearings, Sarbanes announced:

> My concerns on these fundamental questions of the limits on constitutional power which General Haig would draw and his perceptions with respect to the use of power under our unique form of government remain too strong for me to be able, in good conscience, to support the nomination.[14]

The committee approved Haig by a vote of 15–2. Dick Lugar, by then a member of the committee, voted with the majority. The full Senate consented to the nomination by 93–6.

General Haig lasted eighteen months as secretary of state. His determination to be the "vicar" of American foreign policy offended the teamwork orientation of Reagan's White House staff, and the public was offended by Haig's televised breathless assertion that he was "in charge" at the White House while President Reagan lay on the operating table, shot by John Hinckley, on March 30, 1981.

Sarbanes was soon on the trail of a less prominent Reagan appointee on behalf of Maryland residents employed by the federal government. Donald J. Devine, a political scientist at the University of Maryland and a campaign worker for Reagan since 1976, was appointed as

director of the Office of Personnel Management (OPM). Devine pro-
claimed his displeasure with the "excessive pay, benefits, and prerogatives of federal employees."[15]

Reagan budget cuts resulted in the firing of six thousand federal
workers in the national capital area. Devine airily stated that the Reagan
target of eliminating seventy-five thousand federal jobs could be easily
accomplished, particularly with the scheduled abolition of the Depart-
ments of Energy and Education.[16] In August, Devine had ordered a 6.5
percent health benefits cut in insurance plans offered federal workers by
two unions. In October, a U.S. district judge found his action illegal. In an
unrelated case, another judge found Devine's direction to insurance companies that they should not provide coverage for abortions to be unjusti-
fied on budgetary grounds; rather, his action was "ideological" in nature.[17] The OPM had been politicized.

Paul Sarbanes felt that Devine had treated loyal and talented career
civil servants like mortal enemies. He joined two Maryland Democratic
congressmen in calling for Devine's resignation.[18] Senate supporters of
the Reagan administration were riding high in 1981 and were not inclined to listen to Democratic complaints about its political appointees.
In 1985, when Devine's term expired, Sarbanes' opposition prevented
Devine's confirmation for a second term. This provides an example of the
summary judgment by a noted student of the federal government: "Probably more executive branch officials have been fired or reassigned as a result of pressure from the Congress than by the president."[19]

Sarbanes undertook another rear guard action in behalf of the Baltimore Public Health Service Hospital. The Reagan administration decided
that these hospitals should be financed locally or not at all. The Maryland
and Baltimore governments developed a plan to provide state and local
finance, but it would not be in place when the federal grant was due to
expire. Sarbanes appeared before the House Appropriations Subcommittee to plead for an interim appropriation for such hospitals which would
allow an orderly transition and avoid disbanding the staff.[20]

Sarbanes developed a critique of Reaganomics in speeches in Maryland, on the Senate floor, and in committee hearings. Much of this latter
work was done in the Joint Economic Committee (JEC). He held a series
of hearings in Maryland concerning the impact of high interest rates, particularly upon small businesses. Since the JEC has no legislative responsibilities, these activities consisted of "position taking," rather than legislat-
ing. Theoretically, the groundwork might be laid for future legislation. At
least a voice was added to the public discussion.

In 1982, interest rates were the immediate source of pain. But Paul Sarbanes' critique involved all of Reaganomics. He said so that summer.

> The press is treating this thing as though there's some magic idea out there that's gonna solve the economic problems . . . [T]here's not some bright light that's gonna go on. That's Kemp-Roth, from the other side; now what do you want, a Democratic equivalent of Kemp-Roth, to get us into as much difficulty as that got us into? . . . Should some of the domestic programs be cut? Yes, the tree ought to be pruned. It ought not to be chopped down at its roots, which is what this crowd is trying to do . . . They've given away so much of the revenue base, they're projecting large deficits even when they assume that the economy will be working at or close to full employment.[21]

The Political Context Changes Again

The election of 1986 brought back a Democratic majority to the Senate but did not smooth the way for Democrats to regain the White House. The electorate saw George Bush as the right person to conserve Reagan's economic gains; 1988 was a prosperous year. Divided government tended, in the Senate, to push reasonable disagreement over the line into unreasonable conflict. But Senators Sarbanes and Lugar continued to focus on the possible, seeking legislative accomplishment.

Within twenty-eight months, Chairman Paul Sarbanes and the Democratic majority of the Joint Economic Committee published an obituary for Reagan–Bush prosperity. On March 21, 1991, the committee's annual report listed three enduring long-term sources of economic weakness: growth of debt in all economic sectors, the stagnation of real wages, and the concentration of income growth in the wealthiest fifth of the nation's families. These trends combined to make the economy vulnerable. Short-term shocks converted economic growth into recession following Iraq's invasion of Kuwait. The shocks were a rapid rise in oil prices and the collapse of consumer confidence due to the uncertainties of probable war.[22]

Uncomfortable with the growing national debt, President Bush negotiated a treaty to reduce the deficit with Democratic congressional leaders in a 1990 "budget summit." Bush approved $150 billion of new taxes, which enraged Republicans in Congress and outside. After the House of Representatives rejected the plan, a hasty second version of the agreement was passed on October 27. The November Congressional election primarily returned incumbents; the Republican position was not improved. President Bush's attitude toward Congress became increasingly confrontational.

The Senate Foreign Relations Committee fared poorly after the Democrats reclaimed the Senate majority. Chairman Claiborne Pell of Rhode Island found himself incapable of forging a useful synthesis between the Democratic doves, hawkish Republicans, and unpredictable Jesse Helms, the ranking minority member. Pell yielded to urgings of Democratic committee members to give the subcommittees authority to draft legislation.

As chair of the International Economics Subcommittee, Sarbanes took charge of the biennial foreign aid authorization bill. Adapting foreign aid to the realities of a multipolar world was a process unlikely to attract public attention or stimulate public enthusiasm. The proposed International Security and Economic Cooperation Act of 1991 was reported out of the full Foreign Relations Committee by a vote of 17–2, with Dick Lugar's support. Bipartisanship was featured in cooperative floor leadership of the bill, with Sarbanes joined by Republican Mitch McConnell of Kentucky.

Democrat Paul Simon of Illinois successfully sponsored a floor amendment which provided $20 million of the bill's $28 billion for support of the United Nations Population Fund, which supports family planning worldwide. The bill attracted a veto-proof majority of 74–18.[23] President Bush vetoed the bill because of its support for family planning. The House of Representatives failed to override the veto, so no override attempt was made in the Senate.

Meanwhile, Sarbanes moved toward reform of the unemployment insurance system. Intended as a countercyclical instrument which would immediately replace some income of persons losing their jobs, the system is mainly funded by the federal government but administered by the states. Congress had established an Extended Benefits Trust Fund so that job benefits would continue beyond the standard twenty-six weeks. But the administration failed to use these resources, despite a surplus accumulated in the fund. Paul Sarbanes led several colleagues in sending a letter to President Bush seeking increased funding so that the states would be able to speed up the response to applications.[24] The effort finally succeeded with Bill Clinton in the White House.

Another theme of the Joint Economic Report was the inadequacy of monetary policy to bring the recession under control. In their fixation on the dangers of inflation, the Federal Reserve Board held interest rates higher than was consistent with economic recovery.[25] Because of the 1990 budget agreement, Congress could not manipulate fiscal policy by cutting taxes or by increasing spending. Monetary policy determined by the independent "Fed" was the only major tool available to curb the growing recession. Sarbanes introduced a bill to remove the twelve regional Federal Reserve Bank presidents from membership in the policy-making committee, reducing them to the status of advisers.

Sarbanes formed an alliance with Senator Jim Sasser of Tennessee, chairman of the Senate Budget Committee, to launch a campaign for economic stimulus. Their proposed remedy was

> [a] temporary program of grants and/or loans to state and local governments, a middle-class tax cut and a further extension of unemployment benefits [to] provide quick and effective countercyclical stimulus. State and local governments would be able to stave off further tax hikes and spending cuts, a middle-class tax cut could be structured so that its impact is felt immediately and unemployment benefits put money directly into the hands of consumers in areas hardest hit by recession.[26]

While Paul Sarbanes consolidated his committee and subcommittee positions around his expertise in economics, Dick Lugar developed his role as a Republican spokesman on foreign affairs. He presented George Bush a copy of his 1988 book on foreign policy, *Letters to the Next President,* which the then vice president received graciously. Responding to a question in the Vice Presidential Debate, Dan Quayle named Lugar's as one of three "very important" books he had read during the previous six months.[27] When Bush settled into the White House, Lugar became a frequent visitor and adviser.

Forced into second place on the Foreign Relations Committee by Jesse Helms' assertion of seniority, Dick Lugar replaced Helms as the senior Republican on the Agriculture Committee. He forged an alliance with the Democratic chairman, Senator Patrick Leahy of Vermont, to draft the 1990 farm bill. After six days of debate, the bill was passed by the full Senate. By forming a coalition of Republicans and antisubsidy Democrats, Lugar first defeated a move to peg farm price supports to the inflation index and then helped achieve a historic change in farm policy, cutting $3.5 billion from program costs, and giving the farmer more decisions to make, with fewer assigned to bureaucrats.[28]

As American agriculture became increasingly consolidated, with larger, more mechanized farms operated by a smaller farm population, the Department of Agriculture steadily became larger and more special- ized. In Marion County, Indiana, a farmer could not do his business with the Agriculture Department by visiting a single location, since the various subdivisions of the department maintain separate field offices. Dick Lugar's investigators reported that 179 local field offices spent more on overhead than they disbursed in farm subsidies.

Lugar launched an attack on the nation's sixth largest government organization in 1991.[29] As a Republican senator demanding new econo- mies from a department led by Republicans, Lugar's concern could not be dismissed as partisan politicking. However, when George Bush failed to win a second term, the players in the game changed dramatically.

His concern for agriculture did not distract Indiana's senior senator from national security issues. Lugar teamed with Democratic Senator Sam Nunn of Georgia to focus bipartisan attention on the danger of the thirty thousand nuclear weapons still deployed in the former Soviet re- publics. They achieved consensus on a narrow bill to provide aid only for the purpose of storing and then dismantling weapons of mass destruc- tion. The result was a Senate vote of 86–8 granting President Bush au- thority to award $500 million for dismantling nuclear weapons and a vote of 87–7 providing $200 million for an airlift of humanitarian supplies. Lugar and Nunn had demonstrated the ability of Congress to act without presidential leadership in case of a clearly perceived foreign policy need.[30]

Lugar saw that the authorization was meaningless without executive branch action. He criticized President Bush directly for his failure to deal with the issue. When Bush did respond, Lugar found the statement unsatis- factory.[31] He published an op-ed column in the *Washington Post* calling for public vigilance, while again pointing the finger of responsibility at Bush.[32]

Adaptations

The proximate influence on legislative behavior is the political environ- ment or context. The legislator must adapt to changed circumstances or risk his career. Ronald Reagan entered the presidency with a more coher- ent message and staff than Lugar and Sarbanes had experienced with Jimmy Carter. His electoral victory was also more clear cut. Circum- stances combined to make the new president more powerful and Con- gress more pliant. Sarbanes and Lugar both voted for the final version of

President Reagan's budget. Voting similarities between their adaptations to Republican electoral victory did not end at that point. Dick Lugar used his new status as chairman of the relevant subcommittee to introduce an interest subsidy bill fervently supported by the housing industry. As a jobs bill with the best chance of avoiding a veto, it passed with bipartisan support, including that of Paul Sarbanes. But the veto came, and it was sustained by the House of Representatives.

Marked changes in the two senators' roll-call voting coincided with their 1982 reelection campaigns. Dick Lugar's 1982 decline in the indexes of party unity and conservative coalition support proved not to be temporary. When I asked Lugar about this in 1992, he responded that his inclination was to vote with either President Reagan or President Bush when members of their party were deserting them. This claim is supported by Lugar's stellar record of presidential support. But not every party unity or conservative coalition vote is one on which the president has taken a position. Dick Lugar's classic conservative concern for preserving the organic society led him to positions that, in recent years, have not always been shared by his Republican colleagues.

Paul Sarbanes and Dick Lugar played different senatorial roles after 1981 than they anticipated on entering the chamber in 1977. Rather than climbing the seniority ladder of a confident majority party, Sarbanes found himself in the minority, no longer leading a subcommittee to conceive legislation. Instead, he fought rear guard actions to protect Maryland interests from the ravages of Reagan's budget cuts. Lugar suddenly belonged to the Senate majority, faced with the responsibility of governing. The conservatism he espoused seemed to be sweeping all before it, yet the first fruits of a conservative economic policy brought distress to Indiana and the nation; Lugar had to oppose President Reagan's determination to "stay the course."

Partisan fortunes were again reversed in 1986, when Democrats regained the Senate majority. The strains of divided government were renewed, but the careers of both Lugar and Sarbanes progressed smoothly in the 102nd and 103rd Congresses. Ironically, Lugar's legislative initiatives in farm legislation and dealing with leftover Soviet nuclear weapons were more successful in a Congress nominally controlled by the Democrats than were Paul Sarbanes' initiatives in economic policy. Lugar's successes were marked by bipartisan consultation, as was Sarbanes' work on reforming foreign aid, which was nullified by Reagan's veto. But Sarbanes' remedies for the recession did not win unanimous Democratic support, while they stimulated intense Republican opposition.

Dick Lugar came to the Senate in 1977 as a member of the minority party. He developed the habit of bipartisan compromise in order to achieve legislation. Paul Sarbanes tended to see the Democratic party as the vehicle of governance, or at least of accomplishment in the Senate, and he was not used to reaching out to the Republicans.

Notes

1. James L. Sundquist, *The Decline and Resurgence of Congress* (Washington: Brookings Institution, 1981).
2. Interview with Senator Sarbanes, April 15, 1992.
3. Interview with Keith Buhlen, September 12, 1982.
4. Campaign Notes column, "Lugar, Willing to Be No. 2, Touts Baker," *Washington Post,* June 16, 1980, p. A7.
5. Interview with Senator Lugar, August 28, 1980.
6. The decisions of 1981 and their aftermath are described in David Stockman's confessional memoir, *The Triumph of Politics* (New York: Harper and Row, 1986). For a brief, more objective account, see Lou Cannon, *President Reagan: The Role of a Lifetime* (New York: Simon and Schuster, 1991), chapter 12. For the story of the program's fate in the Senate, as seen by the chairman of the Budget Committee, see Richard F. Fenno, Jr., *The Emergence of a Senate Leader: Pete Domenici and the Reagan Budget* (Washington, D.C.: Congressional Quarterly Press, 1991). For a scholarly account of Reagan's budget policies, see Paul E. Peterson and Mark Rom, "Lower Taxes, More Spending, and Budget Deficits," chapter 7 of Charles O. Jones, ed., *The Reagan Legacy* (Chatham, N.J.: Chatham House Publishers, 1988).
7. Stockman, *The Triumph of Politics,* p. 147.
8. R. Douglas Arnold, *The Logic of Congressional Action,* pp. 178–181.
9. All quotations from the Senate floor are from the *Congressional Record* for the appropriate date.
10. Quoted from U.S. Government Printing Office, "Report by the Committee on Banking, Housing, and Urban Affairs on the Emergency Mortgage Interest Reduction Payments Act of 1982, April 2, 1982." Senate, 97th Congress, p. 2.
11. Interview with Senator Sarbanes, July 5, 1982.
12. The veto message is in the *Congressional Record,* House of Representatives, June 24, 1981, p. H 3919.
13. Interview with Senator Lugar, May 26, 1992. For the multiplier effect, see John Maynard Keynes, *The General Theory of Employment Interest and Money* (London: Macmillan, 1954), p. 115.
14. Quotations are from U.S. Government Printing Office, "Hearings before the Foreign Relations Committee . . ." Senate, 97th Congress.
15. Peter M. Benda and Charles H. Levine, "Reagan and the Bureaucracy," in Charles O. Jones, ed., *The Reagan Legacy,* p. 130.
16. Kathy Sawyer, "Personnel Aide Sees Cutbacks through Attrition, Retirements," *Washington Post,* September 26, 1981, p. A14. The story accompanied a front-page feature on the human cost of the federal "reduction in force" then under way.

17. Laura A. Kierman, "Federal Workers' Benefit Cuts Ruled Illegal," *Washington Post,* October 11, 1981, p. B7.

18. "Insensitive Don Devine Asked to Quit OPM Post," *Federal Times,* June 7, 1982, p. 3. Cited by Louis Fisher, "Congress and the Removal Power" in James A. Thurber, ed., *Divided Democracy* (Washington, D.C.: Congressional Quarterly Press, 1991), p. 263.

19. Harold Seidman, *Politics, Position, and Power* (New York: Oxford University Press, 1980), p. 54. Quoted by Louis Fisher in Thurber, ed., *Divided Democracy,* p. 255.

20. See "Hearings on the Department of Labor, Health . . . Appropriations for 1982," Subcommittee on Labor, Health and Human Services, and Education of the Appropriations Committee, Part 3, p. 869. House, 97th Congress.

21. Interview with Senator Sarbanes, July 5, 1982.

22. Senate, 102nd Congress, 1st Session. "The Joint Economic Report" (Washington: U.S. Government Printing Office, 1991), pp. 7–16.

23. *Congressional Record,* July 24–26, 1991; Helen Dewar, "Senate Approves Foreign Aid Bill That Reverses Antiabortion Policy," *Washington Post,* July 27, 1991, p. A13.

24. Stewart Banner, "Nation's Unemployment Insurance System Called Ripe for Major Overhaul," *Annapolis Capital,* May 19, 1991, p. B1.

25. "The 1991 Joint Economic Report," pp. 27–31.

26. Jim Sasser and Paul Sarbanes, "Steps toward Recovery," *Washington Post,* January 13, 1992, p. A17.

27. The Vice Presidential Debate transcript, *New York Times,* October 6, 1988, p. B20. The other two books were Richard Nixon's *Victory in 1999* and Robert Massie's *Nicholas and Alexandra.*

28. Guy Gugliotta, "Lawmakers Agree to Major Agriculture Cuts," *Washington Post,* October 14, 1990, p. A7.

29. Guy Gugliotta, "Lugar Pushes Agriculture Dept. Cuts," *Washington Post,* May 13, 1992, p. A11.

30. George Leopold, "Congress Weighs Move to Aid Soviet Denuclearization," *Defense News,* November 25, 1991, p. 10; Don Oberdorfer, "First Aid for Moscow: The Senate's Foreign Policy Rescue," *Washington Post,* December 1, 1991, p. C2.

31. Mary Curtius, "Lugar Raps U.S. Response to Soviets," *Boston Globe,* December 19, 1991, p. 30.

32. Richard G. Lugar, "A Crucial New Year's Resolution: Start a Daily Countdown of the Number of Soviet Nuclear Weapons Destroyed," *Washington Post,* December 23, 1991, p. A19.

CHAPTER 8

Reelections

Renewing Constituency Ties

The model of influences on senatorial choice asserts that the relationship between the representative and the constituency is central to the politician's craft, and the way that relationship is established and maintained depends on the individual's personality and apprenticeship in which the craft was perfected. The relationship is a continuing one, but the constituency may be in the background of influences determining senatorial actions in Washington. This relationship is in the foreground when the representative returns to visit the constituency, and it explains the entire focus of the campaign for reelection.

The ideal form of that relationship has been defined by Richard Fenno:

> [C]onstituent trust [is what] every representative ultimately seeks to achieve. Trust is that benefit of the doubt or that predisposition to believe which, when held by a large enough number of constituents, keeps representatives secure in their job and free to exercise a good deal of personal judgment in performing it.[1]

The senator's first election may not establish such trust, since the principal electoral judgment may have been a negative one directed against the predecessor. Voters would implicitly place the representative on probation for the first term. More than thirty years ago, Donald R. Matthews studied the 180 persons who served in the U.S. Senate during the decade after World War II. In concluding his book, Matthews described a typical "life cycle" for senators. He designated election to a second term as the critical point in Senate careers. Having survived that test, a senator's election to a third, and often a fourth, term was very probable.[2]

Paul Sarbanes and Dick Lugar fit this pattern. Their first reelections attracted challengers who were experienced politicians and believed the incumbents were vulnerable. Sarbanes seemed vulnerable to those believing that Ronald Reagan's election signaled a conservative and Republican trend; Lugar seemed vulnerable because the immediate result of President Reagan's policies was a severe recession. But the most significant change from their first to their second senatorial elections was the change from challenger to incumbent candidate. Matthew did not emphasize this factor; in the 1950s, incumbents were easier targets. Twenty-eight of thirty Senate incumbents who ran in 1982 were reelected. One reason is that incumbents find campaign funds much easier to acquire.

"A Good Man for Tough Times"

Even before Senator Lugar introduced his interest subsidy bill, the reelection campaign began in Indiana. With no campaigns for governor or president in 1982, the Indiana Republican party placed Dick Lugar's reelection at the top of its agenda. Lugar would provide the help of his coattails to other party candidates.[3] But some ambitious Republican activist might not accept this leadership decision, so the first stage of Lugar's campaign was to ensure that no challenger entered the Republican primary. During 1981, Lugar received the endorsement of the Republican chairmen of all ninety-two county organizations and of the then eleven congressional district organizations. These early endorsements discouraged potential Republican challengers.

The campaign's budgetary target was set at $2.8 million on the basis of expenditures by the senatorial candidates in 1980: Republican Dan Quayle (the winner, spending $2.4 million) and Birch Bayh, the incumbent Democrat, who lost in the Reagan landslide despite expenditures of $2.8 million. Lugar's campaign organization appointed finance directors in each county, and highly publicized fund-raising receptions were held in some forty counties. Nearly a million dollars flowed into the campaign chest a year before the election. This early financial activity, preempting sources of campaign donations, also discouraged potential Republican challengers.

Throughout the campaign, Dick Lugar's Democratic opponent,

Floyd Fithian, charged that Lugar's campaign was supported by political action committees, many from outside the state, representing special interests which were usurping attention Lugar should have paid to Indiana. The Lugar camp responded that the legal maximum PAC contribution of $5,000 was insignificant in a campaign budget of nearly $3 million and that PAC contributions made up but 21 percent of Lugar's funding, while they supplied 50 percent of Fithian's support. (Using percentages obscured Lugar's financial advantage; the total PAC contributions received by Lugar were at least double those made to Fithian.) Republicans intoned that, both in Indiana and nationally, 80 percent of gifts made to the GOP came from donations of $25 or less, while 80 percent of Democratic donations came from donations of $500 or more.[4] Apart from the occasional fat cat Democrat, Republicans had more money to give.

The funds purchased a state-of-the-art media campaign. Television ads in January and February featured Lugar at his Washington desk, working hard. In April, a series of commercials prepared for the spring primary election campaign (although Lugar had no opponent) featured the campaign's permanent slogan, "Dick Lugar: A Good Man for Tough Times."

At the end of June, slick two-minute spots were produced for showing during the summer which combined pictures of the senator listening to constituents or playing the piano for senior citizens, biographical excerpts, testimonials, and shots of Lugar running alone on a track in brilliant red shorts and blue shirt. The new campaign song, written and produced in Nashville at a cost of several thousand dollars, was featured.

> (Refrain)
> If anybody can, Indiana can,
> I'm a-tellin' you a story true,
> If you're ever in a fix and you had your pick,
> You'd want a Hoosier helpin' you.
> (Sample Verse)
> We've got our problems, and we hurt,
> But we're not gonna sit and stew,
> Takin' bulls by the horns
> Is what Hoosiers love to do.

One of the elements in constituent trust is identification; the representative should be seen as "one of us." Lugar had disdained "putting hayseed in my teeth" during his first campaign against Birch Bayh, but his 1982 song exploited the state nickname, and biographical segments

124

identified him, quite truthfully, as an Indiana farmer, businessman, and the father of four sons. They did not mention his affiliation with the Republican party.

The August spots began with the declaration "Jobs are the issue" and showed Lugar with various citizens who had been helped by his efforts—a former union president, a Chrysler plant manager, and a farmer. One depicted Lugar with a building contractor; Lugar expressed regret that his housing bill (identified by the announcer as the only antirecession measure to pass this Congress) had been vetoed but promised to try again—"until we get the job done."[5]

Lugar's Democratic opponent was determined by the May 4 primary election. He was Floyd Fithian, a former associate professor of history at Purdue University, who had nimbly represented Indiana's very Republican second district. Indiana's House representation was reduced from eleven seats to ten after the 1980 census. Unable to recapture Fithian's seat in a fair fight, Republican state legislators divided the district among the neighboring Republican congressmen.

By midsummer, Fithian repeatedly claimed that adequate funds were being denied him. It was an old story. Fithian needed an expensive media campaign to increase his name recognition; but he could not raise the funds to finance that effort until increased name recognition should show that he had a chance to win.

Rather than be charged with fearing to face Fithian, Dick Lugar participated in one debate with his challenger. (Senator Birch Bayh agreed to one debate when Lugar challenged him in 1974.) The only charge Fithian made which affected public opinion in Indiana was his claim that Lugar was an enemy of social security. Fithian became part of a national Democratic effort to use the troubles of the social security system, which both parties recognized, against the Republicans. The solutions proposed by Fithian and Lugar were nearly identical, and Lugar's argument that the fund's troubles resulted from inflation caused by Democratic spending had little effect.[6]

Dick Lugar won with 54 percent of the vote, defeating Floyd Fithian by a margin of 150,000, and leading the Republican ticket by approximately 70,000 votes. He carried all but eight of Indiana's ninety-two counties. One of the eight was Lake County, the home of Gary's steel mills; seven were areas settled by travelers from Kentucky, South of the old National Road. Lugar's coattails were mildly impressive. Republicans retained majorities in both state legislative chambers. Indiana's congressional delegation, which included six Democrats and five Republicans before Fithian's district was abolished, became split evenly with five congressmen of each party.

In a press conference one day after the election, Senator Lugar attributed his victory to the efficiency of the Republican organization, particularly the volunteer effort that reached some 400,000 voters by telephone and letter during the final week of the campaign.[7] Despite the artistry and expense of Lugar's media campaign, old-fashioned personal contact by his supporters contributed significantly to victory.

The Dilemmas of Campaign Finance

Since the days of city machines and party bosses, Americans have suspected that money signals corruption, at least on the part of the opposition. Waves of concern over the role of money in politics have modified American political practices, even as expensive mass communications technology has made the role of money ever more crucial in campaigns

The shady financial activities of Richard Nixon's Committee to Reelect the President were illegal at the time, but they stimulated yet another episode in the American effort to purify our political process. In 1974, Congress made sweeping revisions of the Federal Election Campaign Act which attempted to limit the political advantage of mere wealth. Public funding of presidential campaigns was provided, if the campaigns limited their expenditures. The Federal Election Commission was established as a six-member regulatory body. In congressional elections, strict requirements for reporting campaign contributions were established, and rigid limits were imposed upon the amounts that could be spent by committees, parties, and individual candidates. Political action committees (PACs) were recognized as legitimate channels for campaign contributions.

The law was immediately challenged in the courts. The U.S. Supreme Court struck down nearly all limits on spending as in conflict with the free speech guarantees of the First Amendment.[8] The Court prohibited any limit on the use of their own money by individual candidates in their own campaigns. The Court specified that "independent" political action committee expenditures on behalf of candidates or causes may not be limited. Frank J. Sorauf states the matter succinctly: "'Money talks' was elevated from popular saying to constitutional principle, and the power . . . to regulate campaign finance was thereby severely narrowed."[9]

Paul Sarbanes said that the 1974 law, which he supported in the House of Representatives, should have included a nonseverability clause, because the reforms were adopted as a package. Voiding any part of the law would then have nullified the remaining provisions.[10] Instead, selective invalidation by the Court undermined the law's purpose. A "membership" PAC (established by a union, say, or a corporation) may donate only $5,000 to a primary and another $5,000 to a general election campaign. Although the PAC was invented by organized labor, the number of PACs linked to corporations grew from 89 in 1974 to 1,204 in 1980, while the union PACs increased from 201 to 297 during the same period.[11] "Independent" PACs, which have no parent organization and are allowed to raise money from the general public, have a license to roam the political landscape at will. They may give to an individual candidate without limit as long as their efforts are in no way coordinated with the candidate's campaign.

The reporting requirements of the 1974 law were usually followed, and the Federal Election Commission soon gathered the most comprehensive data of any democratic nation on the origin and disposition of campaign funds. Journalists approached this data bank with the traditional populist assumption that contributions purchase the legislator's vote. They found that, indeed, legislators receiving the largest contributions from a particular PAC often voted in accord with its policies, and many concluded that PACs pose a threat to democracy. In fact, PACs tend to give to candidates who are already supporting the PAC's cause. They support incumbents because incumbents are the most certain investment. In return, PACs expect the legislator's rapt attention when making the case for their position. The history of American campaign finance reform shows that the money always finds its way to the politicians. Abolishing PACs would make the dollars much harder to trace.

The activity of independent PACs, which intervene in campaigns without the consent of particular candidates, increased markedly in 1980. The most famous operator was the National Conservative Political Action Committee (NCPAC), which spent $4 million (raised through direct-mail solicitation) on negative media campaigns against six U.S. senators and claimed credit for defeating four of them, including Indiana's Birch Bayh, defeated by then congressman Dan Quayle.

This success was somewhat illusory, as the candidates NCPAC attacked were liberal Democrats in traditionally Republican states when Ronald Reagan headed the Republican ticket. But the NCPAC leadership was emboldened, and early in April 1981, NCPAC announced its targets for the 1982 elections. At the top of the list was Senator Paul Sarbanes of Maryland.

"Paul Sarbanes: Working for Maryland"

Paul Sarbanes believes that governing cannot be separated from campaigning, since campaigning is communication with constituents, and representation of the constituency is basic to government, regardless of the election calendar. "You can't take politics out of politics," Sarbanes says, "and I don't think you ought to try." He feels that the usual election campaigns are too long; it is hard to stimulate voters' interest months before Maryland's fall primary election. NCPAC's negative TV ads appeared early in April of 1981, forcing Sarbanes into an unannounced campaign. He cooperated with the journalists who reported and criticized NCPAC's invasion of Maryland, and he stepped up his schedule of appearances in Maryland.

A bipartisan group called Marylanders for Fair and Honest Elections was formed to combat the tactics of NCPAC and the other groups which joined the fray against Sarbanes. This apparently independent group could say things about NCPAC's tactics that would have been dismissed as "mere politics," coming from Sarbanes. Liberal Democrats from around the nation rushed to Sarbanes' defense. Their most frequent action was to organize a fund-raising dinner in honor of NCPAC's targeted victims. Sarbanes eventually attended some two dozen of these affairs outside Maryland.

The campaign budget goal was set at $1.5 million, nearly double Sarbanes' expenditure of $891,000 in winning his first term in 1976. By election day in November, the goal was attained. One kind of contribution reflected approval of Sarbanes' voting record. Substantial contributions came from some forty labor union PACs and from groups such as San Franciscans for Good Government. One branch of the Rockefeller family contributed significantly through admiration for Sarbanes' record on environmental issues. Supporters of Sarbanes' dovish foreign policy views provided significant support. The Council for a Livable World, a Washington-based group which favored nuclear disarmament, contributed "less than $50,000" to his campaign.[12] The council operated as an independent PAC, so there was no limit upon its contribution. Liberal organizations were quick to follow the lead of NCPAC and similar groups into "independent" operations, but they were late entering the direct-mail contribution wars.

A second kind of contribution was more a tribute to Sarbanes' status than to his policies. He received $2,500 from the E.F. Hutton Company and a like sum from the Merrill Lynch PAC—goodwill contributions by the stockbrokers for an incumbent member of the Senate Banking Committee. Other contributions came from individuals with Greek surnames, reflecting the senator's continuing support by the Greek-American community, and from prominent Maryland Democrats. Periodic computer-directed mail solicitations brought small contributions from about thirteen thousand individuals.[13] By the end of the campaign, Sarbanes' expenditures slightly exceeded the $1.4 million combined expenditures of his opponent's campaign and NCPAC's "independent" effort. Sarbanes managed to turn NCPAC's intrusion to political and financial advantage.

The campaign shifted into high gear on the long Fourth of July weekend, utilizing Independence Day parades. In three days, Paul and Christine Sarbanes appeared in ten parades in suburban communities including areas Sarbanes had served as a congressman. Years of retail politics had made many residents into friends and supporters. A greeting would be called out from the crowd, and Sarbanes would respond with the constituent's first name.[14]

The Republican candidate was former congressman Larry Hogan, the county executive of Prince George's County. Campaign donations were hard for Hogan to find. The difference was made up by NCPAC. During the September primary campaign, NCPAC ran television spots favoring Hogan. Although the standard disclaimer was flashed on a bit of the screen—"not authorized by any candidate or committee"—viewers assumed they were Hogan ads.

As the campaign warmed up, Sarbanes initiated his own media campaign. The first Sarbanes commercials were designed to contrast with NCPAC's productions. An opening scene showed Sarbanes talking about unemployment against a backdrop of the eloquently smokeless smokestacks of the steel mills of East Baltimore. A slogan flashed on the screen: "Paul Sarbanes: Working for Maryland." This advertisement contrasted with the NCPAC efforts in technique as well as length. Its feature was Sarbanes himself, talking with conviction about the disasters of Reaganomics. It did not use the fancy split screens, dissolves, and other visual devices of the NCPAC ads. The approach was artfully simple: to credit the voter with some intelligence, and to let Paul Sarbanes perform as his own best salesman. Sarbanes acted on his conviction that NCPAC should not be opposed with NCPAC's own tactics.[15]

Sarbanes debated Larry Hogan on TV and was so pleased with the outcome that he debated Hogan five more times on radio and television. Bruce Frame, Sarbanes' press secretary, said that the debates did not attract large audiences but provided leads for journalists covering the campaign.

Senator Sarbanes and Governor Hughes continued the time-honored Maryland practice of providing walk-around money to party workers in Baltimore. Technically, this means paying helpers on election day to shepherd voters to the polls, call on neighbors on behalf of the candidate, and the like. And the practice in this technical sense has been made illegal. The Sarbanes campaign hired consultants and rented cars and equipment from party members in the wards and precincts, with payment in advance of election day. The typical "consultants" would be a state legislator or city councilor or Democratic central committee member who had won a September primary campaign in the same neighborhood. Visiting the neighbors in November, on behalf of Paul Sarbanes, the worker could allay any negative feelings that might have been aroused by the NCPAC media blitz. Since the voters were strongly Democratic in their inclinations, personal contact by a Democrat they had supported in the primary election persuaded them to vote as well in the general election.

Sarbanes' financial support from outside the state, inspired by the NCPAC attacks, was particularly strong. In contrast to the strong parties of Indiana, the Sarbanes campaign made contributions to elements of the Baltimore Democratic organization, instead of receiving financial support from the Maryland party.

On election day, Paul Sarbanes led the Democratic ticket, winning more votes and carrying one more county than Governor Hughes. Sarbanes carried twenty of the twenty-three counties and won Baltimore City by nearly 80 percent. Sarbanes won 63.5 percent of the two-party vote. He won 69 percent of the vote in Prince George's, Larry Hogan's home county.

Paul Sarbanes headed NCPAC's priority hit list of fourteen incumbent members of Congress. Only one of the fourteen was defeated in November. The organization spent more in its campaign against Sarbanes than any other 1982 target. Sarbanes' response showed how to counter such attacks: formulate a nonpartisan third force to critique the intruder's actions; do not attempt to counter the negative campaign by using negative tactics. The margin of Sarbanes' victory was increased by classic tactics of political organization: identify your own vote and get it to the polls. Like Dick Lugar in Indiana, Paul Sarbanes was helped by the old-fashioned endeavors of volunteer supporters.

In 1982, Dick Lugar spent $2,757,573 winning 54 percent of Indiana's vote. His Democratic challenger, Floyd Fithian, was able to spend only $870,023, in contrast to expenditure by then incumbent Democratic senator Birch Bayh of $2,773,254 (while losing) in 1980. In Maryland, Paul Sarbanes spent $1,623,533 winning 63 percent of the total. His Republican opponent, Larry Hogan, reported expenditures of only $90,976. The apparent 16–1 Sarbanes advantage shrank dramatically with the spending, more against Sarbanes than it was pro-Hogan, of nearly $800,000 by the National Conservative Political Action Committee.

1982 marked the pinnacle of NCPAC activities. The independent PACs, which can raise money from anybody, were revealed as money-making enterprises which devoted more of their income to fund-raising and administration than to helping candidates. After 1986, the activities and donations of all independent PACs declined, as less complicated methods of circumventing campaign spending limits, such as "soft money" donations, were developed. But the negative, attack campaign advertising developed by NCPAC and its brethren has become the campaign norm.

Their first reelection campaigns established patterns resulting from the different personalities and apprenticeships of Lugar and Sarbanes. Both would follow the same paths in 1988 and 1994, despite quite different political contexts. Dick Lugar would begin early, preempting party and financial support, to prevent a rival champion rising from the Republican ranks. He would grant a single television debate to his Democratic opponent. Lugar would mount effective, wholesale media campaigns, emphasizing his identities as farmer, businessman, and fifth-generation Hoosier. His typical campaign action would be to deliver a speech to an organization's lunch or at a campaign rally.

Paul Sarbanes would continue to delay his formal campaigns until he was sure that voters might be paying attention. He would continue to practice retail politics in his constituency between campaigns. Maryland is smaller in area and slightly smaller in population than Indiana, which helps make retail politics possible, and Sarbanes' personality is well suited to the task. Despite its smallness, Maryland's geography and population are quite diverse; it has been called "America in miniature." There is no Maryland identity to match Indiana's Hoosier; Sarbanes' campaigns would be based on an appeal to the common man, showing Paul

Sarbanes as merely one of the people, even if better educated than most. His signature campaign action would be to listen attentively to a constituent in the midst of a crowd.

Contesting for a Third Term

Preparing to launch his 1988 campaign, Dick Lugar won the endorsements of county chairmen and lined up major financial supporters. No Republican candidate opposed Lugar for the party's nomination. There were signs of a Democratic resurgence in the state, and the Democratic nominee, Evan Bayh, son of former senator Birch Bayh, eventually won the gubernatorial contest. But no experienced Democrat was willing to take on the uphill task of challenging Lugar.

A novice candidate eventually volunteered. He was forty-one-year-old attorney Jack Wickes, whose only experience was as state campaign manager for Gary Hart's successful 1984 Indiana presidential primary campaign. Wickes declared his senatorial candidacy in September 1987, and won the Democratic primary the following May without opposition. In August, an Indianapolis *Star* survey showed 69 percent favoring Lugar, with 18 percent for Wickes.[16]

With the party nomination in hand, Wickes searched earnestly for campaign funds. The search led only to frustration; Wickes was never able to assemble enough cash even to advertise on television. Lugar did grant his customary single debate, so Wickes was not entirely frozen out of the medium. The candidates agreed on opposing tax increases; they disagreed on abortion and defense policy. Wickes attacked Lugar's high-profile activity on the Foreign Relations Committee, claiming that Lugar was more concerned with international issues than with the problems of Hoosiers, imitating the tactic that helped defeat several former chairmen of the Foreign Relations Committee. Wickes prefaced specific charges with such statements as "If Richard Lugar was as familiar with the problems of the people of Gary as he is with Guam . . ." Each time he repeated the rhetorical device, Wickes named a different city. Lugar said the tactic was irrelevant and that he had visited each of the named cities for twenty years.[17]

In November, Lugar's actual vote was only 1 percent less than his support in the August newspaper poll. He won with 68 percent of the statewide vote. He erased traces of the Civil War from the Indiana electoral map by carrying 91 of 92 counties. The lone holdout was Lake County, a Democratic area since the New Deal. Lugar won 8 percent more votes than the Bush–Quayle ticket. If Bush's choice of the junior Indiana senator as running mate pained him, Lugar did not show discomfort.

Unlike Indiana, where the permanent political party organizations can all but determine which candidates will enter primary elections, Maryland at the beginning of the political season is a circus of individual ambitions. Two perennial, minor candidates entered the Democratic lists against Paul Sarbanes. Republican party leaders tried unsuccessfully to enlist a celebrity candidate, and nine Republicans paid the $290 qualifying fee to run for the Republican senatorial nomination.[18]

The winner of the Republican primary withdrew in a few weeks, seeing no hope for adequate party support. The Republicans named Alan L. Keyes as their candidate. A former Reagan administration State Department official, Keyes was a passionate neoconservative who had just taken up residence in Maryland. Keyes eventually gathered some $600,000. Sarbanes' war chest held $1.5 million.

Keyes pursued the same will-o'-the-wisp as NCPAC six years before. The opposition's thesis in both elections held that Paul Sarbanes is a leading liberal, yet Maryland is a conservative state. A *Washington Post* reporter summarized the result.

> The campaign offered perhaps the nation's clearest choice between an unapologetic liberal and an aggressive neoconservative . . . [T]hey clashed on many of the positions Sarbanes has taken . . . abortion . . . economic sanctions against South Africa . . . "Paul Sarbanes believes we should take power out of the hands of the people at the bottom and put it into the hands of a centralized government," Keyes declared. . . . Sarbanes responded, "I don't accept the proposition that the government is the enemy of the people. Government is the instrument of the people."[19]

Sarbanes tried to swing Maryland's electoral votes behind his Harvard Law School classmate Michael Dukakis. But the disasters Dukakis suffered in the national campaign were as visible to Marylanders as to the rest of the nation. The alliance between blue-collar workers and country club Republicans initiated by Ronald Reagan was continued for another election. George Bush carried Maryland by less than 50,000 votes out of 1,702,000, winning 51 percent to 48 percent for Dukakis.

Paul Sarbanes scored a personal triumph. His total vote was 999,166, just shy of a landmark victory: no Maryland candidate had ever won a million votes. Voter turnout was greater in a presidential election year, and Sarbanes' vote increased by 292,000 over his 1982 total. Yet this represented about the same share of the vote. In 1982, Sarbanes won 63 percent of the two-party vote; six years later, he gained 62 percent. As in 1982, Sarbanes carried every Maryland county except three less densely populated jurisdictions in traditionally Republican western Maryland. He won 11 percent more votes than Bush. Sarbanes could argue that he, not Bush, won any mandate awarded by the Maryland voters. His dismay at the tactics of the Bush campaign reinforced Sarbanes' conviction that the Democrats' approach, particularly to economic policy, represented the true public interest and was endorsed by Maryland's voters.

Campaigns for a Fourth Term

Midterm elections are often dominated by local issues, and the president's party normally loses a few seats in Congress. The 1994 election was nationalized through the efforts of Newt Gingrich's House Republicans, who publicized their Contract with America. Republicans gained fifty-two seats in the House and eight in the Senate. Against this backdrop of impending national change, Paul Sarbanes and Dick Lugar traveled familiar campaign paths. The initial stage of the contest was easy for both men. Dick Lugar had no opponent in the spring Republican primary and Paul Sarbanes had no serious opponent in the September Democratic primary.

Winner of the Democratic nomination to challenge Dick Lugar was Jim Jontz, an able Democratic politician who had been elected to Congress three times as representative of one of America's most Republican districts in the Indiana heartland. The district elected Jontz because he was the most attractive candidate and reelected him despite a rather Democratic voting record. However, Jontz played a leading role only on Democratic issues that did not impact his district. For example, he became a leading House champion of the spotted owl, a species threatened with extinction by lumbering in Washington and Oregon.

In 1992, Jontz lost his House seat to Stephen Buyer, an army reserve captain outraged by Jontz's vote against participation in the Gulf War. When the voters no longer paid attention to talk of the war,

Buyer imported timber workers from the Northwest to testify that over-protection of the spotted owl's habitat was costing union jobs.

Jim Jontz was a more believable challenger than nearly unknown Jack Wickes had been in 1988. Wickes never achieved enough support to finance television advertising; Jontz provided ads which attracted national notice. They dramatized the perennial claim that senators concerned with foreign affairs must forget the home folks and played on resentment against foreign aid financed by American taxpayers. The typical ad showed Jontz by the city limits sign of an Indiana town like Peru, Moscow, or Lebanon. He would announce that Lugar had provided millions for the town's namesake; an actor playing "local resident" would respond that none of the money had been seen in those parts.[20]

Despite humorous television spots, Jontz's candidacy remained a long shot and his financial support remained uncertain. As usual, Lugar agreed to a single TV debate. Both candidates were articulate and the debate was inconclusive. However, to support his claim that Lugar's international interests led him to neglect Indiana, Jontz challenged Lugar to promise that he would serve a six-year term if reelected, and not seek some other office, such as the presidency. Lugar replied that he had never regarded his Senate position as a stepping stone, but he also never made promises that might foreclose future options. From that point on, any reference to Jontz's ploy at a Lugar campaign rally led to a chant from the audience: "Go for it!"[21] Hoosier Republicans found the prospect of a Hoosier president quite acceptable.

Lugar's campaign spent $3.5 million by mid-October. Given the political circumstances of 1994, Lugar's eventual victory was hardly in doubt; only its magnitude was in question. Lugar's total campaign expenditures exceeded Jontz's by a ratio of ten to one, but Jontz's campaign kept Lugar's vote total slightly below the 68 percent he won in 1988. Lugar repeated his 1988 triumph of carrying ninety-one of Indiana's ninety-two counties. In winning 67.3 percent of the vote, Lugar became the first Hoosier to win more than a million votes in an election. His total was 1,039,625 votes.[22]

Paul Sarbanes' Republican opponent was William Brock, heir to a candy manufacturing fortune, an experienced politician with serious liabilities. Brock's experience as an elected official consisted of three terms in the U.S. House of Representatives and one term as a senator from Tennessee. Defeated for reelection to the Senate, Brock became chairman of the Republican National Committee and then served Republican presidents in various positions, including secretary of transportation. Marylanders have been sensitive to the political pretensions of outsiders since the Civil War. Sarbanes did not label Brock a carpetbagger, but he did remind voters that Brock began paying Maryland income taxes only in 1990. Brock would have been the first person in the twentieth century elected to the Senate from two different states; several politicians made successful second starts in the West in the nineteenth century. Brock's somewhat unfocused campaign never caught fire. He loaned $1.8 million to his own campaign and raised $1.4 million from other sources.

Sarbanes activated his computer files of supporters, worked the Greek-American organizations, and accepted generous donations from financial industry PACs. Sarbanes was slated to become chairman of the Banking Committee if, as expected, Democrats retained a Senate majority. The PACs were eager to clinch the ability to argue before him for their preferred policies. Their contributions totaled $230,000, compared to $26,700 provided by the same sources in 1988. When Sarbanes was asked if this would create a conflict of interest, he assured questioners that he retained the ability to make independent judgments.[23] Sarbanes supported reform legislation that would have limited Brock's ability to bankroll his own campaign as well as Sarbanes' ability to win support from the interest groups. But he had to seek reelection under the laws of 1994.

Sarbanes practiced retail politics, meeting and greeting voters wherever they gathered. Opinion polls awarded Sarbanes such a commanding lead that editors did not regard the campaign as newsworthy and did not send reporters to cover its events. Reporters who did turn up were amazed at the contrast with neighboring Virginia, where the campaign between former lientenant colonel Oliver North and the incumbent Democrat, Charles Robb, was tracked by national as well as local media.[24]

Social scientists are seldom able to conduct experiments in the manner of their colleagues in the physical sciences. Yet the variation in Paul Sarbanes' campaign funds over the years may be compared to his vote totals as proof that, while a critical minimum amount of funding is a prerequisite, money alone does not win elections. When he won a second term in 1982, Sarbanes' opponent had substantial support from the National Conservative Political Action Committee. Sarbanes still outspent his opponent and NCPAC combined by $200,000; and he won 69 percent of the vote. In 1988, Sarbanes' opponent, Alan Keyes, suffered from campaign poverty; neither the Republican party nor organized groups nor wealthy individuals saw fit to provide him with the funds that, at least in theory, could have made him competitive. Sarbanes outspent Alan Keyes by $803,000 and won by 68 percent. In 1994, Sarbanes' wealthy opponent,

William Brock, outspent him by $434,000, yet Sarbanes won 59 percent of the two-party vote. In no instance was there a clear connection between dollars spent and votes won.

By a large margin, Sarbanes carried the most populous jurisdictions, Baltimore City and Prince George's County. He carried the same counties as in 1988, becoming the second Marylander to be four times elected to the U.S. Senate. Maryland elected Democratic Senator Millard Tydings to a third term in 1938 over the opposition of President Franklin D. Roosevelt and to a fourth term in 1944. The contrast between the conservative Tydings and liberal Paul Sarbanes measured half a century's change in Maryland politics.

The Reelection of Incumbents

From the senators' point of view, the ideal outcome of an election campaign is to reinforce the trust which constituents place in their representative. For the purpose of understanding senatorial actions, however, even greater significance attaches to the impact of their campaign experiences on the candidates themselves.

In all three of these contests, Senators Lugar and Sarbanes were incumbents enjoying the advantages of incumbency. Winning a second term was a milestone in their careers; elections seemed easier thereafter. Any election may return an incumbent, but the incumbent will not be quite the same person who began the campaign.

> [P]olitical campaigns may leave their mark on American politics less by changing the officeholder's face than by influencing the officeholder's thinking—and the perceptions and behavior of challengers, activists, reporters, and others as well. In this important way, campaigning is a vital component of the linkage between political leaders and the public.[25]

Reelected senators have more influence and elicit more respect. People have higher expectations of them. At the same time, the reelected senator has an increased store of self-confidence, fresh from the renewal of his endorsement by the state's electorate. Both Sarbanes and Lugar won by margins made more comfortable by financial advantages over their competitors. Part of their renewed sense of security came from confirming their ability to raise campaign funds. And, of course, the irony:

their margins of victory were so comfortable that they could ignore marginal changes in constituent opinion. Perhaps the constituents' sense of trust in their representative is so rewarding to all concerned that agreement between them on specific policies takes a back seat.

Notes

1. Richard F. Fenno, Jr.: *When Incumbency Fails: The Senate Career of Mark Andrews* (Washington, D.C.: Congressional Quarterly Press, 1992), p. 11.
2. Donald R. Matthews, *U.S. Senators and Their World* (New York: Vintage Books, 1960), pp. 241–242.
3. Interview with Gordon Durnil, Indiana Republican State Chairman, July 8, 1982. Sixty percent of Indiana voters then cast their ballots on voting machines; the vote they cast for the head of the ticket tripped every lever in that party column. To vote for the opposition candidate for another office required raising the tripped lever and lowering the opponent's lever.
4. State Chairman Gordon Durnil quoted these figures in an interview on July 8, 1982. Dick Lugar repeated the same figures in a Lincoln Day Dinner speech in Terre Haute, Indiana, that evening.
5. This description of Lugar's ad campaign is based on a videotape produced by Bailey, Deardourff and Associates, "Lugar for Senate Compilation Reel," 1982.
6. Patrick J. Traub, "Lugar, Fithian Focus on Social Security Issue," *Indianapolis Star*, October 10, 1982, p. 4B.
7. Patrick J. Traub, "GOP Credited for Fashioning Lugar Victory," *Indianapolis Star*, November 4, 1982, p. 21.
8. *Buckley et al. v. Valeo*, 424 U.S. 1 (1976).
9. Frank J. Sorauf, *Inside Campaign Finance: Myths and Realities* (New Haven: Yale University Press, 1992), p. 11. Also see Cass R. Sunstein, "Free Speech Now," in G.R. Stone, R.A. Epstein, and C.R. Sunstein, eds., *The Bill of Rights in the Modern State* (Chicago: University of Chicago Press, 1992).
10. Interview with Senator Sarbanes, July 4, 1982.
11. These are January, 1981, figures from the Federal Election Commission, reported in Roger H. Davidson and Walter J. Oleszek, *Congress and Its Members* (Washington: Congressional Quarterly Press, 1981), p. 360. For a study of the nonprofit, untaxed independent PACs which emphasizes their unregulated nature and their connection with profit-making businesses, see the series of investigative reports by Robert Timberg appearing in the *Baltimore Sun*, July 11–25, 1982.
12. David S. Meyer, *A Winter of Discontent: The Nuclear Freeze and American Politics* (New York: Praeger, 1990), p. 243. Meyer says it was "disingenuous" for the group to claim a major role in Sarbanes' overwhelming victory.
13. The detail quoted here is from C. Fraser Smith, "Big Name Firms, Far-Away Areas Helped Sarbanes Campaign," *Baltimore Sun*, February 8, 1983, p. A4. The author visited the direct-mail operation at Sarbanes' Baltimore headquarters in September 1982.
14. The author rode in the parades with Paul and Christine Sarbanes on July 4 and 5, 1982.

15. This description of the Sarbanes ads is based on a videotape supplied by the producer, Concept Associates of Baltimore.

16. Doug Richardson, "Lugar, Wickes to Debate in Senate Race," Associated Press release, September 9, 1988.

17. Doug Richardson, "Lugar, Wickes Debate in Senate Race," Associated Press release, September 10, 1988.

18. Robert Barnes, "9 in GOP to Oppose Sarbanes," *Washington Post*, December 29, 1987, p. C1.

19. Robert Barnes, "Sarbanes Crushes Keyes for 3rd Term in Senate," *Washington Post*, November 9, 1988, p. A40.

20. One of Jontz's ads was shown and praised by Charles Bierbauer on "Newsmaker Saturday," October 22, 1994. See CNN transcript #246.

21. Interview with Senator Lugar, December 16, 1996.

22. Mary Dieter, "Million-Vote Man, Lugar, Sets Another Hoosier Mark," *Louisville Courier-Journal*, November 10, 1994. Final vote total given from Michael Barone and Grant Ujifusa, *The Almanac of American Politics, 1996* (Washington: National Journal, 1995), p. 474.

23. Charles Babington, "PACs Are Banking on a Sarbanes Win," *Washington Post*, November 2, 1994, p. D6.

24. Charles Babington, "Brock, Sarbanes Race Quietly toward Tuesday's Finish Line," *Washington Post*, November 3, 1994, p. C1. Robb eventually won with 46 percent to North's 43 percent and independent candidate Marshall Coleman's 10 percent. North raised and spent $20 million; Robb spent $5.5 million. More than money was involved in Virginia.

25. Marjorie Randon Hershey, *Running for Office: The Political Education of Campaigners* (Chatham, N.J.: Chatham House, 1984), p. 31.

CHAPTER 9

Reaching for Policy Goals
The Advantages of Leadership Position

The impact of election campaigns upon constituents is important; more important for explaining senatorial actions is their impact on the senators. Reelection by a comfortable margin gives the legislator renewed self-confidence. His or her policies are now newly endorsed by the voters. Without slighting constituency needs, the senator is more free to pursue personal ambition, or even the national interest. Senators Sarbanes and Lugar returned from their second-term elections to seek increased leadership responsibility.

The thread that connected their different endeavors was their concern for public policy. They did not pause to savor increased power for its own sake. They utilized whatever resources came to them to achieve policy goals. A core ingredient of the political context when determining choice is the position held by the senator in the Senate hierarchy. Each reelection meant new status as they took actions to solidify the advantages of increased seniority. Finally, in 1996, Dick Lugar tried for the supreme prize, the presidency.

After election to his second term, Dick Lugar sought an organizational position with no official concern for policy. This was in keeping with his status as a product of the strong Indiana party organization. He won the chairmanship of the National Republican Senatorial Committee (NRSC), an important channel for funding the reelection efforts of incumbent Republican senators, regardless of their ideological leanings.

The NRSC distributed an account of Lugar's 1982 reelection as a model for Republican incumbents seeking reelection in 1984. The document emphasized the need to plan, organize, and raise funds early, before an opposition (either within or outside the party) has a chance to close ranks. As a source of cash contributions (largely collected as "soft money" unlimited in amount because not designated for individual candidates), national party committees such as the NRSC add to the advantage enjoyed by incumbents. Dick Lugar testified before the Senate Committee on Rules and Administration when it conducted one of the frequent but fruitless investigations of campaign finance. He defended the political action committee "movement" as being itself a reform movement which provided many small contributors with a method for joining with likeminded others to make a political impact. "It is," he said, "the antithesis of back-room politics."[1]

Paul Sarbanes had testified before the same committee, but he told a different story. Fresh from his defeat of NCPAC, he declared that "[t]he independent PACs operate outside the framework of accountability and simply become hit artists on the political scene."[2] Lugar spoke as the temporary fund-raiser for Republican incumbents, while Sarbanes drew on bitter campaign experience.

An area which many senators have regarded as practically immune to constituency opinion is foreign affairs. Dick Lugar is a convinced internationalist; since Indiana Republicans have a history of isolationism, some political risk was involved when Lugar supported American activities abroad. His Democratic opponents in both 1988 and 1994 claimed that international questions distracted Lugar from dealing with Indiana's problems. Neither opponent made significant progress, indicating that the trust Lugar has built with his constituents is strong and constant.

Senator Sarbanes in Opposition

The power of the purse gives Congress the ability to determine priorities in America's relations with other nations. Historically, the Foreign Relations Committee has authorized foreign aid. But the effectiveness of the committee declined from its pinnacle in the Fulbright era, until it was unable even to win passage of a foreign aid authorization bill by the full Senate. President Reagan bypassed the group to win needed funds directly from the House Appropriations Committee and the Senate Finance Committee. Paul Sarbanes' actions in the realm of foreign affairs were taken both within and outside the committee, which he joined in 1977.

The joint House and Senate investigation of the Iran-Contra scandal was a reassertion of Congress's constitutional role in determining foreign policy. Sarbanes' appointment to the investigative committee resulted from his reputation for careful preparation and impartiality, his judicial temperament.

On the fourth day of the hearings, Sarbanes summarized the testimony of retired air force major general Richard V. Secord. The tangled tale included using government help to raise money and buy arms for privately chosen military projects. Sarbanes told Secord, "[y]ou've constructed an arrangement whereby you can go outside any channels of accountability, any normal channels of procedure."[3]

A few days later, the riveting testimony began of Lieutenant Colonel Oliver L. North of the National Security Council staff. North cheerfully explained the need to operate covert operations in a manner that would give his superiors "plausible deniability." The uniformed North was admired for standing up to the panoply of congressmen arrayed against him in the hearing room. North said he got permission for covert operations from his supervisors, the two successive heads of the National Security Council, retired marine lieutenant colonel Robert C. McFarlane and rear admiral John Poindexter. In his final admonition to North, Sarbanes called up the Constitution.

> [T]he essence of our constitutional system . . . is that it gives us a process by which we can resolve these sharply held differences amongst ourselves. And we have to maintain that process. The substantive goal does not justify compromising the means we have put into place.[4]

Paul Sarbanes was appalled that men like McFarlane, Poindexter, and North calmly advertised their indifference to, or ignorance of, the basic nature of the U.S. Constitution; they lacked a schoolboy's understanding of the document. All three were graduates of the U.S. Naval Academy in Annapolis. Sarbanes was a member of the Naval Academy's Board of Visitors, a civilian group appointed half by the president and half by the congressional leadership, which serves some functions of a board of trustees. Both West Point and the Air Force Academy taught required courses in U.S. government and the Constitution, but the Naval Academy did not require such study. Sarbanes recommended that the Academy fill this curricular void. When his suggestion was not taken very seriously by the Academy administration, he quietly helped arrange for $5 million of the Academy's annual appropriation to be temporarily withheld. The Academy administration suddenly paid rapt attention to the need for midshipmen to understand the Constitution they swear to uphold.[5]

In 1989, Paul Sarbanes launched a crusade from his Foreign Relations Committee seat that scored success by attracting media attention. Sarbanes was dismayed when President Bush made his first ambassadorial nominations. Despite the 1980 Foreign Service Act, which states that the post of chief of mission should normally go to career Foreign Service officers, Bush was nominating twice as many political appointees. The sole qualification of several seemed to be their large contributions to the Republican party.[6] Sarbanes argued that the sole criterion should be the competence of the nominee to represent the United States in that particular country. The realization that one could buy an ambassadorship, he stated, demeaned all American ambassadors.

One of the nominees drawing Sarbanes' ire was Joseph Zappala of St. Petersburg, Florida, nominee for ambassador to Spain. Mr. Zappala was a real estate developer, spoke Italian, and had wanted to become ambassador to Italy. He had donated over $100,000 to Republican causes in 1988. When asked on the official Foreign Relations Committee questionnaire to list any special qualifications he might have, Mr. Zappala answered, "I am known as a coalition builder. I am able to organize my colleagues and peers to action in support of worthwhile civic, charitable, and political causes."

This answer interested Sarbanes because of the way another real estate developer from St. Petersburg, Melvin Sembler, nominated to be ambassador to Australia, answered the same question: "I have been known as a coalition builder, able to organize my colleagues and peers to action in support of worthy civic, charitable, and political causes." Mr. Zappala's public relations consultant completed the questionnaire with a copy of Mr. Sembler's responses, completed by Sembler's public relations consultant, before him.[7] The Committee divided along party lines to recommend the Zappala nomination by a one-vote margin.[8]

Sarbanes' opposition to the nomination of Joy Silverman was harder to refute. Silverman, a New York socialite, was nominated for ambassador to Barbados and other Carribean island nations. Her husband, finding the ambassador's residence inadequate, rented a second Barbados home, prior to the Senate's consideration of the nomination. Ms. Silverman offered "no foreign policy experience, no job history and no college degree,"[9] and Paul Sarbanes' questioning revealed that she was ignorant of the Caribbean drug traffic. The Senate sent the nomination back to the White House; Silverman asked the administration not to resubmit her name.[10]

Paul Sarbanes succeeded in making the qualification of ambassadorial nominees a political issue. Beyond the daily press, articles about ambassadorial qualifications appeared in *Time, Newsweek, Harper's,* and *People.* Sarbanes' challenges of Bush nominees ended when the administration began sending nominations Sarbanes considered reasonable to the Foreign Relations Committee.

Senator Lugar Uses the Freedom Awarded by the Voters

Dick Lugar was better positioned than Paul Sarbanes to assert leadership within the committee structure. A greater turnover among Republican senators meant that the length of Lugar's service, identical to Sarbanes', boosted him further up the seniority ladder. Lugar obtained a seat on the Foreign Relations Committee when a vacancy occurred after the 1978 election.

When the Republicans won the Senate majority in 1980, Charles Percy of Illinois became chairman of a badly splintered Foreign Relations Committee. The Democratic members favored disarmament, a nuclear freeze, and a cautious foreign policy. Most of the Republicans took opposite positions. The third-ranking Republican, Jesse Helms of North Carolina, fought the administration over the appointments of ambassadors and advocated a foreign policy all his own. Howard Baker, the second-ranking Republican, was absorbed in his duties as majority leader. Senator Percy was retired by Illinois voters in 1984, and Baker retired of his own volition the same year. When the Republican caucus met to organize the new Congress in 1985, Lugar's campaign to succeed Baker as majority leader was derailed by his colleagues' clear desire that Lugar move ahead of Helms to become the chairman of Foreign Relations.

Lugar wanted to restore the committee to its former prestige. He saw that this could only be based on bipartisanship. He launched two months of hearings which he defined as a search for consensus. He quickly turned to the agenda items urged by Claiborne Pell, the senior Democrat on the committee. In accord with Pell's wishes, Lugar then guided the Senate to ratification of the United Nations–initiated treaty proscribing genocide, which had been before the Senate for thirty-nine years. Ratification had always been blocked by a few senators expressing concern for American sovereignty.

The committee discussed specifics of the 1985 foreign aid authorization bill. The Foreign Relations Committee had been bypassed in the process of determining foreign aid for the previous five years. Committee members shared Lugar's desire to restore committee influence, and they maintained a quorum throughout an eleven-and-a-half-hour markup session on March 25. The bill was debated by the full Senate in mid-May and passed, 75–19. With the bill's passage, the morale of members and staff of the Senate Foreign Relations Committee soared.

Meanwhile, Lugar established good working relations with the Reagan foreign policy apparatus. He convinced the administration to twice postpone a request for $2 billion in military aid for Jordan. In November 1985, President Marcos announced a snap election for the Philippines and invited American observers. President Reagan asked Lugar to lead the 20-member American delegation.[11]

At poll closing time in Manila on Friday, February 8, 1986, Lugar told reporters that he personally had observed no fraud. This interview was repeated throughout the evening by Philippine government-controlled media to assure voters that the election was being conducted honestly. When the observation team gathered in Manila Saturday evening, it became clear that its various groups had observed quite different elections, depending on the location. Lugar became convinced that Marcos was delaying the count to determine how many fictitious votes to claim for himself. When the team departed as scheduled, Dick Lugar read a careful farewell statement which praised the dedication of the many voters but deplored the increasing reports of irregularities in the counting and tabulation of the results.[12]

Both Marcos and Corazon Aquino proceeded on the assumption that they had won. For Aquino, this meant holding mass street meetings to protest Marcos's theft of the election. Filipinos responded with revolutionary fervor. The crucial opinion was Ronald Reagan's. After hearing Lugar's report from the front lines, Reagan answered a press conference question by stating that fraud had apparently occurred on both sides. Dick Lugar then took his case to the American public on television, leading a bipartisan effort to change Reagan's mind. Finally, Marcos received the fatal word from President Reagan, via Senator Paul Laxalt, that he must resign. Against his will, Ronald Reagan had been led into a notable foreign policy success.

Many conservatives accepted without challenge the assertions of right-wing authoritarian rulers who claimed the only alternative to themselves would be communism. The American government then supported anti-communist dictators, to the dismay of their subjects. Dick Lugar perceived that American interests would be safest in a world containing as many democracies as possible: both authoritarian and totalitarian governments should be undermined. Lugar labeled as the "Reagan Doctrine" a little-noted speech the president gave on March 14, 1986, in which he declared that "the American people believe in human rights and oppose tyranny in whatever form, whether of the left or of the right."[13]

Lugar had already taken on the question of economic sanctions against South Africa. The issue became linked with the question of aid to the Contras of Nicaragua. One group of senators favored economic sanctions against South Africa but would filibuster to prevent military aid to the Contras. Another group favored Contra aid but would filibuster to prevent the application of sanctions against apartheid. Neither issue could be acted upon unless the other were dealt with.

Lugar supported the Reagan position on aid to the Contras. In 1985, he had worked with Georgia Democrat Sam Nunn to prevent another annual renewal of the Boland Amendment, which prohibited aid to the Contras. The result was the Lugar–Nunn Amendment, which provided $27 million in nonmilitary Contra aid. It was passed with a slender majority of 56–43. This compromise between the desires of President Reagan and those of a congressional majority became the first official American help to the Contras since 1983. But the Senate could not act finally on the issue without linked cloture votes to determine that both Contra aid and sanctions against South Africa would be considered—as amendments to a bill raising the limit on the national debt.

The concept of applying economic sanctions against the Union of South Africa to express international displeasure with that nation's system of apartheid gained the adherence of several European nations in the early 1980s. Beginning in 1981, the Reagan administration's South Africa policy was labeled "constructive engagement," which was soon dismissed as a code phrase for American acceptance of apartheid. The Black Caucus of the House of Representatives wanted to sever relations completely between the two nations and require American corporations doing business in South Africa to withdraw.

Dick Lugar led the Foreign Relations Committee in formulating legislation that was milder than what he called the "scorched earth" policies contemplated in the House of Representatives. The bill was finally passed by a vote of 80–12 in July 1985. Secretary of State George Shultz called on Lugar to explain that President Reagan preferred that the executive branch conduct foreign policy. He showed a draft of an executive order that would implement most policies in the conference committee report. If Congress pressed on with the legislation, however, Reagan would veto it.

Lugar and Majority Leader Dole felt that Reagan had accepted so much of the congressional policy that they should simply declare victory and let the matter drop. Lugar approached the Senate parliamentarian and, as chairman of the committee with jurisdiction of the bill, took physical possession of the relevant document and locked it in his office safe. With the document absent from the chamber, it could no longer be considered.[14]

In the ensuing year, the South African situation deteriorated further. Clashes between the government and protesters had claimed 875 lives in 1985. The government then banned television and other coverage, claiming the presence of cameras in the "emergency areas" was an incitement. The rate of casualties was doubling in 1986 without any coverage.[15] On July 12, 1986, the South African government declared a state of national emergency. Troops were sent to occupy and "protect" schools being boycotted by black students.[16]

On July 22, President Reagan gave a speech on South Africa stating that economic sanctions would hurt the very blacks they were intended to help. Dick Lugar concluded that the Reagan administration had changed neither its attitude toward South Africa nor the personnel who administered an irrelevant policy. He held three days of hearings by the Foreign Relations Committee as a prelude to proposing strong new economic sanctions against South Africa.[17]

During markup of the bill, liberal Democrats including Paul Sarbanes proposed more drastic sanctions, and Lugar accommodated them. The bill was reported out by a 15–2 vote. Lugar wanted the sanctions to be real and painful to South Africa, leaving no doubt about American opposition to apartheid. At the same time, the bill should gain the support of more than two thirds of the Congress and thus be veto-proof. On August 15, the Senate passed the amended bill by 84–14.

If the House should pass a different version of the legislation, delayed passage would provide Reagan a perfect opportunity for a pocket veto. The House members overcame their misgivings about Lugar's intentions—misgivings based on his physical removal of the bill from Senate consideration in 1985—and adopted the Senate bill word for word by a vote of 308–77.

On September 16, Lugar met with White House officials and Majority Leader Bob Dole. President Reagan's chief of staff, Don Regan, suggested the same solution as a year earlier. President Reagan would issue the substance of the legislation as an executive order; in return, Dole and Lugar would lead an effort to sustain the Reagan veto. Writes Lugar,

I was deeply disappointed in the Regan offer, since it reflected a naive belief that an executive order could solve the problem in 1986 as it had in 1985 . . . [I]n 1985 . . . I believed that the President should be given the opportunity to implement a new policy approach toward South Africa, but that opportunity was ignored and we found ourselves a year later in the same position.[18]

Lugar called the White House to say that he could not accept the offer. The veto message came on September 26. It was overridden, 313–83 in the House and 78–21 in the Senate. Congress had taken an unequivocal stand, while avoiding the complete rupture advocated by the champions of total divestiture. The Botha regime then in power attempted to ignore the sanctions, but the South African people could not ignore their economic impact. After replacing the Botha government, the de Clerk administration released African National Congress leader Nelson Mandela from prison and began talks which led to a relatively peaceful acceptance of majority rule.

It was fitting that Dick Lugar and Paul Sarbanes, former Rhodes Scholars educated with funds originating in the labor of black South Africans, were active in nudging South Africa toward this outcome. According to Herman Cohen, who was the National Security Council staff member for Africa during Reagan's presidency, Dick Lugar was the hero of the fight for sanctions against South Africa. "The difference," Cohen concluded, "was that Lugar's foreign policy views were not driven by a domestic agenda."[19] Lugar was free to follow his own star in guiding the Foreign Relations Committee.

Despite the vestiges of isolationism in Indiana, the constituent trust Lugar had established allowed him to realize his policy preferences. There were important consequences. Lugar achieved the status of major Republican spokesman in the field of foreign policy. He was called to the Bush White House for consultation as often as three times a week. The media sought Lugar for Republican comment on foreign relations. Lugar retained his bipartisan attitude, seeking allies wherever he could find them. He developed his working relationship with Sam Nunn of Georgia, Democratic chairman of the Senate Armed Services Committee. Several Lugar–Nunn amendments resulted from their association.

When the Democrats gained a Senate majority in the 1986 election, committee chairmanships switched party. Jesse Helms felt that his promise to his constituents to give priority attention to agriculture had been fulfilled, so he claimed ranking minority membership of the Foreign Relations Committee. Although committee Republicans unanimously supported Lugar for the position, Helms prevailed in the full party caucus, where he invoked the principle of seniority.

Dick Lugar turned to the work of the Agriculture Committee with relish, as partially described in chapter 7. Lugar played a lead role in writing and passing the farm credit law of 1987 as prelude to drafting the farm bill of 1990. Probably since his father's tutelage in childhood, Dick Lugar has been hostile to the complex federal subsidy program for major crops, which led some farmers to pay more attention to bureaucratic requirements than to market forces. Lugar's constituent trust in Indiana was so overwhelming that he could ignore any farm faction wedded to the price support program. But the final blow against price supports could not yet be struck. The 1990 farm bill ended payments for taking land out of production, froze target prices and dairy supports, and placed many more decisions in the hands of the farmer.

In 1991, Senator Lugar launched his crusade against the bloated bureaucracy of the Department of Agriculture. In 1995, as chairman again of the Agriculture Committee, he challenged the need for farm subsidies at the confirmation hearing of incoming agriculture secretary Dan Glickman. All of this activity set the stage for the 1996 farm bill.

Senator Sarbanes Wins the Confidence of His Colleagues

The Republican capture of a Senate majority in the 1980 elections made President Ronald Reagan's program possible, with the help of the boll weevil Democrats in the House. Senate majority leader Howard Baker and Robert Dole, his successor, saw Republican unity as the key to effective governance. The key to an effective response was a unified Democratic effort. Senator Robert C. Byrd of West Virginia, mortified to be the minority, rather than the majority, leader, hoped to establish Democratic alternatives to Republican proposals. He looked to Paul Sarbanes for leadership in formulating party positions.

Private meetings of all Democratic senators and a few staff members were held in the Capitol to plan party strategy. Richard d'Amato was one of those staff members; he described Paul Sarbanes' role.

> Sarbanes was the classic, behind-the-curtains strategist. He was a close
> confidant of Byrd . . . He was always great in the inner-party

strategizing sessions. He was always very influential in hammering out and developing the basic strategy as we moved into the legislative process . . . The caucus would meet Tuesdays for lunch, and I was in those luncheons. Sarbanes was somebody you always wanted to hear from. You always wanted to know what Sarbanes thought about it, because he was so bright. His advice was always well considered . . . I can remember times when he would derail a proposal that would have gone, but for his argumentation. He was always very influential. And remains influential.[20]

D'Amato pointed out that Sarbanes invariably came down on the liberal side of a question, but he arrived at the position in reasoned, persuasively argued stages.

A hallmark of the successful inside player is that he doesn't talk about his influence. Sarbanes has never done so. However, his staff does refer inquisitive journalists to others. A *Baltimore Sun* reporter was referred to former senator Thomas Eagleton of Missouri. The interview gave a dramatic picture of Paul Sarbanes at work.

Back when the GOP still controlled the Senate . . . Democrats would sometimes file glumly into their Tuesday lunch in the Capitol, sharply divided over how to respond to a White House initiative.

Thomas F. Eagleton recalls how then-Minority Leader Robert C. Byrd would stand up in the chandelier-lit Lyndon B. Johnson Room, describe the problem and then "sort of glare" at Sen. Paul S. Sarbanes, "as if to say, 'Get up and lead us out of this wilderness.' And Mr. Sarbanes would tick off the options: A, B, C.

"By the time he finished, you knew that A was superb and B and C were disastrous," said Mr. Eagleton. . . "He did it in a marvelously compelling way."[21]

Since entering the Senate in 1977, Paul Sarbanes has been remarkably constant in voting with the Democratic party majority, even as the political climate in the nation and in the world has changed and changed again. Sarbanes votes with the party majority partly because he himself plays a significant role in determining the party position, if there is to be one.

The confidence of the Democratic leaders was demonstrated when Sarbanes was appointed to the first-ever special committee of twelve to try U.S. District Judge Harry Claiborne of Nevada on behalf of the full Senate. The House of Representatives impeached Claiborne, who had been convicted in the courts of income tax evasion but refused to resign. Claiborne began to serve his two-year sentence while continuing to collect his annual salary, since the Constitution's procedure for removing judges from office specifies impeachment by the House and conviction by a two-thirds vote of the Senate.

Beginning October 7, 1986, the full Senate reviewed the case presented by the special committee, found Judge Claiborne guilty, convicted him on three of four charges, and removed him from office.

Sarbanes also tested the confidence of his colleagues in a very public manner. The problem was a Reagan administration initiative intended to get government out of business competition. Two of the three major airports serving the Washington metropolitan area, Dulles Airport in Virginia and National Airport in the District of Columbia, were owned by the federal government. Legislators use National Airport heavily and wanted the facility improved but were hesitant to make the taxpayers foot the bill. The Department of Transportation proposed to sell the airports to a regional authority, which would be able to sell bonds to finance airport improvements.

The third airport serving the metropolitan area is the Baltimore–Washington International airport (BWI), located somewhat nearer to Baltimore than it is to Washington. Senator Sarbanes believed that improvements to the other airports would give them an unfair advantage. Unable to win a commitment of funds for BWI, he organized a filibuster against the bill benefiting the other airports. He enlisted the aid of Republican Charles Mathias, the senior Maryland senator, and Democrat Ernest B. (Fritz) Hollings of South Carolina, interested in some help for airports in his own state.

The filibuster consumed parts of nine days. Sarbanes was careful not to obstruct the Senate's general business, but only the Metropolitan Washington Airports Transfer Act. Political scientist Barbara Sinclair, then conducting research on the Senate, was surprised that none of the respondents she asked about filibusters complained about Sarbanes' effort.[22] When asked about this, Sarbanes described the delicate balance of the operation.

> We never carried it to the point where we would provoke such a reaction, that everyone was just sort of being steamrollered. We had a piece of legislation that the Department of Transportation wanted to get done. And we said, "Well, it's got to get done in a broader context." And we finally got them to perceive the desirability of a broader

context . . . I think it was a piece of good legislative work, and the comment she made just supports me in that point of view.[23]

Sarbanes' Democratic colleagues supported him by initially preventing a successful cloture vote. The filibuster gained attention for the needs of BWI airport. A substantial federal grant supported improvements there, and the metropolitan area quickly developed more than enough business for three first-rate commercial airports.

Achieving Policy in New Contexts

The political context changed in 1992 with the election of Bill Clinton. Washington was busy for the next two years with the Clintons' proposed health care reforms. In 1994, House Republicans came to Washington heralding a revolution that would get the federal government "off the backs of the people," reduce taxes, and restore individual initiative. But only nine of the seventy-three GOP freshmen had ever served in the majority party of a legislature. The Senate did not share their interpretation of the election. Years of partisan drama followed, from the repudiation of President Clinton in 1994, through shutting down government to coerce his acceptance of Republican budgets, a nasty contest for the 1996 Republican presidential nomination, and President Clinton's reelection.

Paul Sarbanes played a supporting role in these dramas, while Dick Lugar reached for stardom when he sought the presidential nomination. Sarbanes was the senior Democrat on the Senate special committee to investigate the Whitewater scandal. The chairman was volatile New York Republican Alfonse d'Amato. Sarbanes' role was to be the Democratic watchdog of the Republican majority's proceedings. His was the face seen next to d'Amato's when the TV evening news gave a few seconds of coverage to the hearings. This service dominated Sarbanes' life, as the special committee held sixty days of public hearings, gathered 274 depositions, heard 159 witnesses and, along with other Whitewater investigations, spent $31 million.[24] The time-consuming task had no direct connection with particular public policies, but the stakes in terms of the Clintons' reputation were substandtial.

Despite advance leaks of expected allegations, the televised sessions never gained a wide audience. After thirteen months of effort, the investigation ended quietly. No wrongdoing by either the president or the first lady, in the White House or in Little Rock, was established by the committee's evidence. Sarbanes was responsible for the minority report, which charged that the majority's practice was "to construct conclusions first and discard the facts as they become inconvenient."[25] An indication of the obscurity of his role was Sarbanes' pleasure at receiving praise from a Georgetown University law professor for the effectiveness of the minority report.[26]

Senator Lugar Tries for the Prize

Since he became an Indianapolis mayoral candidate, Dick Lugar's political career made common cause with the Indiana Republican party. There is no comparable national party able to recruit and nurture presidential candidates; if Lugar aspired to the White House, he had to place his own name in contention and attract favorable media attention, for the news media essentially determine modern presidential nominations.[27] With the "Go for It" cheers of campaign rallies still echoing, the Indianapolis CBS television station released a poll showing Dick Lugar twenty points ahead of any alternate presidential candidate among Indiana voters. In February, Dan Quayle declined to enter the contest, citing family concerns. With no competition for Hoosier campaign support, Lugar could make an Indiana-based presidential run. He felt it was the right time for him, in terms of his experience, particularly in foreign policy, and his physical vigor. With the encouragement of his wife and four sons, Lugar accepted the invitation of New Hampshire Republicans to appear at a gathering of presidential candidates in February 1995, a full year before the New Hampshire primary election.

What of financial support? Senator Phil Gramm of Texas attempted a kind of preemption by announcing that $20 million is required for a serious presidential nomination bid, and that he had raised $25 million. Lugar disagreed, estimating that $5 to $10 million could take a candidate through the early primaries; if he were successful, more support would find him. At the time, Lugar had no inkling that he would face the private millions of Stephen Forbes.

Lugar knew that a year was a short time in which to prepare a presidential bid. Media coverage of Lugar's official announcement of candidacy, at a massive rally in Indianapolis, was blanked out by terrifying news of the bombing of the federal building in Oklahoma City on the same day. The rest of the campaign was an attempt to gain attention for his candidacy and for his ideas. He did not have the funds needed to force himself upon the public through a television advertising blitz.

Lugar's candidacy had a firm base in issues on which he had built a Senate record. He argued that only the president can lead in resolving the two problems which most threaten America: nuclear security and fiscal sanity. The Lugar–Nunn collaboration showed the way to safely dismantling the former Soviet Union's arsenal and combating nuclear terrorism. For the fiscal question, Lugar had proposed, as early as April of 1995, a 17 percent sales tax, with abolition of the federal income tax and the Internal Revenue Service.

Lugar left the campaign trail in Iowa to finish what he began as chairman of the Agriculture Committee. The pending legislation had the happy name, from his point of view, of the Freedom to Farm Act. Lugar had to confront an opposition led by Senator Tom Daschle of South Dakota, the Senate minority leader. South Dakota Democrats have fought for higher farm price supports as for their birthright. The 1996 farm bill, which Lugar fathered, gradually but completely phases out farm price supports in seven years. Farmers will be free to produce for the growing markets abroad.

The primary elections of 1996 were front-loaded. The process begun in mid-February was essentially concluded by mid-March. A serious competitor needed front-loading in terms of money. Lugar raised $5 million and eventually received federal matching funds of $2.5 million. His proposal for eliminating the Internal Revenue Service by substituting a sales tax collected by the states was confused with, and then drowned out by, the $35 million spent by Stephen Forbes to promote his concept of a flat-rate income tax.

When asked about the Supreme Court's ruling on campaign finance, Lugar answered with remarkably good cheer.

> The only way I could have gained equity would have been to have a system in which I could approach wealthy donors, say, five of them, to give twenty million dollars each. I would name the five, so the voters could decide if I was being unduly influenced by them. With that money, I could begin to talk about the end of the income tax, the need for American leadership in the world, and the integrity of government, in a way in which my freedom of speech [would be] enhanced very substantially.[28]

Reporters covering the primary campaigns were more interested in the "horse race" elements of the contest than in issues or candidate qualifications. They wanted to know who was ahead, and from following what strategy. Dick Lugar was the leading Senate Republican spokesman on foreign policy. Instead of reporting his positions on foreign affairs, TV reporters wondered aloud if voters would be interested in anybody's position on foreign affairs.

Dick Lugar placed seventh in the Iowa caucuses with 4 percent of the vote. In New Hampshire, he was fifth with 5 percent. His strongest showing was 14 percent for a fourth place finish in Vermont. He withdrew from the race soon thereafter. Unlike some of his competitors, Lugar survived the experience with both his integrity and his dignity intact. Just as he had refused to "stick hayseed in my teeth" in his first Senate campaign, he never pretended to be anyone other than himself.

Making Use of Their Freedom

Senators Lugar and Sarbanes gained the trust of their constituents through service in Washington, frequent visits in the constituency, and successful campaigns for reelection. This trust gave them freedom from concerns about sudden changes in constituent opinion. Both used the freedom to pursue policy preferences. And they used it in the traditional way, building seniority and expertise on their committees. Dick Lugar was better positioned on the seniority ladder; he served two memorable years as chairman of Foreign Relations, forcing change in Reagan administration policies toward the Philippines and South Africa. He became a recognized Republican spokesman on foreign policy. When Jesse Helms took over Foreign Relations by asserting seniority, Lugar became the senior Republican on the Agriculture Committee and soon was its chairman. He led the Senate to a historic change in farm policy. And his try for the presidential nomination had a sound basis in issues.

Paul Sarbanes used the self-confidence that comes with repeated reelection to solidify his quiet influence in the Senate Democratic party. He scored victories as a subcommittee chairman when the Democrats held the majority; he was blocked from becoming chairman of the Banking Committee when the Democrats failed to recapture a majority. His colleagues recognized Sarbanes' judicial temperament; he served repeatedly on investigative committees where his refusal to take a position without complete knowledge served the national interest. He became chairman of the Joint Economic Committee, which does not propose legislation. He won the extension of unemployment benefits to stimulate economic recovery, and he had the satisfaction of seeing the kind of policies he supported—particularly abstention by the Federal Reserve Board from raising interest rates—associated with a nearly unprecedented national prosperity.

Notes

1. U.S. Congress, Senate, Committee on Rules and Administration, "Hearings on the Federal Election Campaign Act of 1971 . . . ," 98th Congress, 1st Session, May 17, 1983, p. 325, quoted by Larry J. Sabato, *PAC Power* (New York: W.W. Norton, 1990), p. xi.
2. "Hearings," January 27, 1983, p. 159. Quoted in Sabato, *PAC Power*, p. 183.
3. "The Iran-Contra Hearings: Day Four of the Testimony," *Washington Post*, May 9, 1987, p. A13.
4. *Taking the Stand: The Testimony of Lieutenant Colonel Oliver L. North* (New York: Pocket Books, 1987), pp. 580–581.
5. Interview with Professor Charles Cochran, former chairman of the Naval Academy Political Science Department, May 14, 1994. A complex story of five Naval Academy graduates—the trio mentioned here, plus former navy secretary and novelist James Webb and Arizona Senator John McCain—highlighting the strained relations between those who served in Vietnam and those who avoided service, is told by Robert Timberg, *The Nightingale's Song* (New York: Simon and Schuster, 1995).
6. U.S. Congress, Senate, Foreign Relations Committee, *Nomination of Joseph Zappala*, Exec. Rept. 101–14, 101st Congress, 1st Session (1989), pp. 5–7. This committee document gives the most complete history of Sarbanes' crusade against the Bush appointees.
7. The public relations consultants confessed to reporters from the *Washington Post*. Bill McAllister and Paula Yost, "Two Would-Be Envoys Are Frequent Partners," *Washington Post*, June 24, 1989, reprinted as appendix 5 of the committee's report on the Zappala nomination, cited above.
8. Helen Dewar, "Sarbanes Fails to Block Envoys's Confirmation," *The Washington Post*, October 4, 1989, p. A25.
9. Anne Devroy, "Envoys Without Experience," *Washington Post*, July 18, 1989, p. A1.
10. Anne Devroy and Bill McAllister, "White House Surrenders on Envoy," *Washington Post*, Febuary 1, 1990, p. A19. "On the advice of friends in politics, [Silverman] told the White House not to resubmit her name."
11. John M. Goshko, "Lugar to Monitor Marcos Race," *Washington Post*, January 25, 1986, p. A1.
12. The statement is reprinted in Lugar's *Letters to the Next President*, (New York: Simon and Schuster, 1988), pp. 147–148. This account of the election is drawn primarily from Letter Five, pp. 95–148.
13. Quoted in Richard G. Lugar, *Letters to the Next President*, p. 29. In this book, Lugar sets forth the principle of fostering democracy as one which should guide any president of the United States. He recounts the achievements of the Foreign Relations Committee under his chairmanship as demonstration of the theorem.

14. Lugar, *Letters,* pp. 217–222.
15. Lugar, *Letters,* p. 223.
16. Associated Press, "Pretoria to Keep Troops Stationed at Black Schools," *Washington Post,* July 29, 1986, p. A9.
17. Edward Walsh, "Lugar to Urge New S. Africa Sanctions," *Washington Post,* July 29, 1986, p. A1.
18. Lugar, *Letters,* p. 235.
19. Interview with Ambassador Herman Cohen, December 2, 1993.
20. Interview with Richard d'Amato, November 13, 1992. D'Amato is not related to the Republican senator from New York. Beginning in 1980, he was Minority Leader Byrd's principal assistant for defense matters on the Democratic Policy Committee, which d'Amato described as "the minority leader's policy stable."
21. Doug Birch, "Sarbanes Prefers to Work the Details Backstage," *Baltimore Sun,* February 1, 1988, p. 1A (part two of a three-part profile).
22. Barbara Sinclair, *The Transformation of the U.S. Senate* (Baltimore: Johns Hopkins University Press, 1989), p. 96.
23. Interview with Senator Sarbanes, April 15, 1992. Concerned with losing control over the airports, Congress established an advisory commission made up of members of Congress who could overrule decisions of the regional authority. This was attacked as being a form of the legislative veto, found unconstitutional in *Immigration and Naturalization Service v. Chadha,* 103 S. Ct. 2764 (1983).
24. U.S. Congress, Senate, "Final Report of the Committee to Investigate White-water Development Corporation and Related Matters," June 17, 1996, pp. 1 and 399. The majority and minority reports could not even agree on these numbers.
25. Ibid., p. 395.
26. Interview with Senator Sarbanes, December 16, 1996.
27. The story of declining presidential parties and the arrogance of the media is told by Thomas E. Patterson, *Out of Order* (New York: Alfred A. Knopf, 1993).
28. Interview with Senator Lugar, December 16, 1996.

CHAPTER 10

Sarbanes, Lugar, and the Senate

This book began by asserting that six factors influence the outcome of senatorial choice. Critics of Congress argue that other influences are overwhelmed by the corruption inherent in the system. Whatever noble cause initially brought the member to the Senate is forgotten in the self-serving struggle to finance yet another campaign. Votes can be sold to special interests, like souls sold to the devil. In this view, a freshman senator may come to Washington full of reforming zeal and a sense of mission; both are soon fractured on the rocks of reality.

How much adaptation to changing realities should we expect from a senator? We want it both ways; he should profit from experience, but not forget the cause that brought him to the Senate. Does experience in the Senate have a corrosive impact on a senator's world view, his very ideology? I got some clues toward answering such questions when I repeated in 1992 a query I first posed to Sarbanes and Lugar in 1977: what are the two or three most important issues facing the nation?[1]

The two senators agreed with each other far more in 1992 than fifteen years earlier. Although neither knew of the other's response, both named the same general issues, and in the same order. International problems brought about by what Sarbanes called the "implosion" of the Soviet Union were their top priority. Economic issues came second, with Lugar focusing narrowly on the federal budget deficit, while Sarbanes spoke more broadly of an economic hangover resulting from the excesses of the 1980s. Third, both described problems of poverty and race.

The change wrought by fifteen years was most striking in the case of Dick Lugar. In 1977, Lugar had described three aspects of the same question: achieving a balance between freedom and individual initiative, on the one hand, and seeking or requiring equality, on the other. In 1992, the abstract nature of Lugar's 1977 response disappeared.

> The third problem I see is to try to come to grips with what is called the underclass . . . people who are not well connected with the economy or the politics of the country . . . [T]he Hudson Institute [finds that] by the year 2000, workers will need fourteen years of education to be fairly certain of employment . . . Twenty per cent will be existing on the fringes, [open to] problems of crime, poor housing, drug abuse . . .
>
> The approach is not *laissez faire* in this case. There isn't much chance of jump-starting the opportunities for education of . . . persons who are functionally illiterate and don't want to learn to read. Without substantial intervention into the lives of many people, things will largely go from bad to worse. That then jeopardizes or undermines the stability of our society.[2]

The notion of "substantial intervention" seems a great distance from the libertarian ideal. When I asked what he meant, Lugar cited the example of the Mommobile, a van which travels the most desperate streets of Indianapolis, seeking pregnant girls and women to give them immediate prenatal treatment. This helps avoid both stillbirths and the enormous costs of saving premature babies. Charlene Lugar helped raise a million-dollar endowment to finance the enterprise permanently.

Dick Lugar does not mean coercion when he says "intervention." Fifteen years of Washington experience have demonstrated that the torn fabric of society is not necessarily mended by marketplace mechanisms. Whether that represents a corrosion of Lugar's 1977 ideology, as sketched in chapter 6, is for the reader to decide. In 1996, Lugar cited a further example of intervention. It was the school lunch program, supervised by the Senate Agriculture Committee, which he chairs. During the budget battles of the 104th Congress, House Republicans expected to transfer the program to the states, supported by federal block grants, as they planned for welfare programs. Lugar opposed their plan, pointing out that the states had not sought this responsibility and were not equipped to discharge it. But there was another reason.

> I contended that we should maintain a federal school lunch program. There ought to be a universal safety net for children, in nutrition. This was a very controversial position.[3]

This is the kind of attitude that led to Dick Lugar being labeled as a moderate, when compared to the Jesse Helmses and Philip Gramms of the Senate.

Paul Sarbanes expressed in 1992 a concept of the connection between national policy and private economic behavior which held the Reagan administration responsible for later problems.

> It's my perception that, as a consequence of the decade of the eighties, we have had a much more divided society at home than a lot of us think, having been undercut in both economic strength and social strength. I see a lot of social divisions . . . A lot of people profited in the eighties through speculation and through cutting corners. The people who played it straight, sought to be solid producers, got left behind. The movers and shakers and the corner-cutters got ahead. And that's not my sense of the values that should be rewarded.[4]

Sarbanes said that since there is an economic attribute of social harmony, social peace is far easier to obtain if the economy "is on an upswing with an equitable distribution [of the economic gains]." But economic strength by itself does not assure social peace.

> The question of racial, ethnic, and religious harmony is always one of the critical issues in a society as pluralistic and as varied as this one is. And I fault Bush for not recognizing that . . . We've seen this intensification of the racial clash, ethnic clash, and religious clashes.[5]

Both senators' responses were sensitive to the then existing political context. Half a year after these interviews, the election of Bill Clinton to the presidency changed the context dramatically—or so it seemed. Sarbanes' policy desires had long been frustrated by Presidents Reagan and Bush threatening to wield the veto. In 1992, Sarbanes regarded the Democratic party as the most desirable vehicle for governing the nation. In 1993, however, Clinton's experiment in party government brought more frustration. The president's economic stimulus plan was defeated, and his deficit reduction plan was saved from a tie-vote defeat by Vice President Al Gore. Two of Sarbanes' causes, the Family and Medical Leave Act, and extended unemployment compensation, were passed; extended compensation contributed to economic recovery. But the end of divided government did not ensure the end of governmental stalemate. Clinton needed Republican votes to pass the North American Free Trade Agreement (NAFTA), which Sarbanes opposed as a threat to working Americans.

Dick Lugar adapted readily to the change in administrations. His proposal for consolidation in the U.S. Department of Agriculture was adopted as part of Vice President Gore's reinvention of government initiative. His vendetta against farm price supports made progress. Lugar championed NAFTA, although Indiana's manufacturing workers claimed that they would be adversely affected. Both senators received some national media attention; neither became a household name except in their home states.

The Determinants of Senatorial Behavior

The Senate careers of Paul Sarbanes and Dick Lugar are not complete. When they finish their fourth terms, however, Sarbanes will match Lugar's record of serving longer in the Senate than any other person from his state. Reviewing their careers to date, we can reach conclusions of two kinds. The first responds to the question we asked in the beginning: what led these similar men in opposite political directions? The second type draws conclusions about the nature of the U.S. Senate from the narrative of their two careers.

Richard Green Lugar and Paul Spyros Sarbanes were born six hundred miles and a day less than ten months apart. Herbert Hoover was America's president, but Franklin D. Roosevelt was soon inaugurated. Both firstborn sons grew to adulthood as the United States grew to superpower status. Both attended public schools. Both narrowly failed to be elected president of their respective high school classes but enjoyed political success in college. They entered Oxford University as Rhodes Scholars on the same day in 1954, just as they entered the U.S. Senate on the same day in 1977.

Yet these two senators vote on opposite sides of most major issues. Sarbanes is a liberal Democrat, Lugar a conservative Republican with recent moderate tendencies. Because of their many similarities, the influences that make them into political opposites stand out in sharp relief.

Personality. These firstborn sons had strong-willed fathers. Although the sons absorbed the work ethic at a tender age, their nurturing parents gave them a strong sense of self-worth. Secure in their own identities, they took interest in others: the natural gregariousness of the politician, based on a capacity for empathy.

Paul Sarbanes made friends easily in the kindergarten where he learned English, just as he did in reaching a political pinnacle at patrician Princeton. Dick Lugar conquered every outside activity available in high school and college while finishing academically at the top of his class. Both Lugar and Sarbanes scored initial political successes by trying to open restrictive institutions to broader membership. Lugar's targets were the social clubs of Shortridge High; Sarbanes' were the eating clubs of Princeton.

The way they deal with the world and with their constituents differs, just as the methods used in their first substantive political accomplishments differed. Dick Lugar talks to the voters; he depends primarily on his extraordinarily fluent rhetoric for political impact. Paul Sarbanes listens to voters; then he seeks consensus quietly, behind the scenes. Lugar is a very public person but is not really comfortable when glad-handing; Sarbanes is expert at working a crowd, but he shuns the spotlight in between campaigns.

Their personalities are very different, but they both study problems very thoroughly and exhibit a genuine interest in other people. The latter quality is a foundation for the trust placed in them by their constituents.

Ideology. The experiences of a lifetime both modify and reinforce attitudes acquired at an early age. Dick Lugar's economic conservatism, learned first at his father's knee, was made more complex and sophisticated by his study of such authors as the British statesman Edmund Burke, apostle of the organic society. His understanding of how a great nation can accomplish its purposes in the world came from the example of American admiral Arleigh Burke. His conservatism is tempered by a Christian concern for the less fortunate, which also underlies his gregariousness. Thus Lugar's ideology is a conservatism that recognizes the value of certain governmental interventions in society coupled with an internationalism that sees a major role for America in the world.

Party and ideology have been somewhat separate for Dick Lugar. The Indiana parties are famously nonideological, although the Republicans have a history of isolationism. Lugar's student internationalism was nurtured by his stay in England.

Paul Sarbanes believes, quite simply, that a democratic government should be the servant of the people. He shared his father's fervent admiration for Franklin D. Roosevelt and Adlai Stevenson. He attacked Princeton's eating clubs in the name of fairness. Paul learned how government may influence the economy when he studied economics. He saw how public officials translate ideas into results by working with two distinguished lawyers, a federal judge, and economist Walter Heller, then the chairman of John Kennedy's Council of Economic Advisers.

Sarbanes believes that America must remain a land of opportunity, as it was for his family, for all its citizens, regardless of race or creed. Seeing that the marketplace is a harsh environment, he supports government regulation to ameliorate the random human tragedies of capitalism.

Constituency. Like many senators, Sarbanes and Lugar represent their native states. They absorbed their states' traditions and attitudes as they were growing up. Paul Sarbanes repeated in his own life the theme of Maryland's political history: the striving of socially marginal groups to win equal political participation and economic opportunity. Sarbanes upset the Maryland tradition of electing only wealthy notables to the U.S. Senate. As a second-generation Greek-American, Sarbanes understands the needs of those who seek access to the full benefits of citizenship. He has a natural affinity for the persons who made up the original New Deal coalition: working people, immigrants, farmers, minorities, and intellectuals. He carefully represents the interests of Maryland's people and their greatest natural resource, the Chesapeake Bay.

Maryland is a remarkably diverse state, geographically, economically, and demographically. In offering an identification that will build trust with his constituents, Sarbanes depicts himself as simply one of the people.

Dick Lugar grew up in Republican surroundings. The Civil War first solidified Indiana's partisan preferences; Great-grandfather Lugar, resplendent in his Union officer's uniform, graced the home of Dick Lugar's youth. Marvin Lugar despised the New Deal and Franklin D. Roosevelt, even shielding his family from all but conservative political commentary. The family was involved in the manufacture of baking machinery and raising corn, hogs, and soybeans. Lugar helped persuade conservatives to support a federal bailout of the Chrysler Corporation. He later became chairman of the Senate Agriculture Committee and helped free farmers from burdensome regulation—and the help of price supports. Farmers and businessmen are his natural constituents, yet he believes that many Hoosiers support him because of his adroit legislative maneuvers in the realm of foreign affairs.

In building identification as a basis of constituent trust, Lugar portrays himself as a farmer, a businessman, the father of four sons (and now several grandchildren), and a Hoosier.

Party, Apprenticeships, and Political Styles. Both Lugar and Sarbanes absorbed party identification from early childhood. Sarbanes' father, an immigrant Greek, was a follower of Franklin D. Roosevelt and a Democrat. Lugar's father was a Roosevelt-hater and a Republican; and Great-grandfather Lugar helped Lincoln save the Union. It is as impossible to imagine Sarbanes as a Republican as it is absurd to envision Lugar as a Democrat. Their lives have been spent in their respective parties.

Paul Sarbanes canvassed Baltimore row houses as a reform candidate for the Maryland House of Delegates just as the old, patronage-oriented and corruption-prone Democratic party was being modernized. His was a classic retail political campaign. His ability to withhold judgment pending examination of the evidence made him an insurgent leader in the state legislature, just as it won respect when he served on the House Judiciary Committee during the Watergate crisis. He wields political influence by reasoning with colleagues in private. Although he makes no effort to keep his name and face perpetually before Maryland voters, he is a fiercely effective campaigner. He prefers retail politics, but he has mastered the wholesale skills. He is particularly effective in television debates.

Having won a seat on the nonpartisan Indianapolis school board, Dick Lugar was recruited by the Indianapolis Republican party to run for mayor. As a beneficiary of Indiana's strong, patronage-oriented two-party system, he formed a symbiotic relationship with the Republican organization. Running for mayor or running for president, his style is rhetorical. Public speaking, more than private persuasion, is his primary route to political accomplishment. He is a man of the lectern, or even the pulpit. Awkward when locker room-style camaraderie is called for, he is comfortable before the television cameras and performed well from the beginning in wholesale politics. As a speaker, his primary appeal is to reason, not emotion.

Policy Preference. "Preference" is too mild a term for the convictions a politician may hold on certain subjects—Justice Douglas, for example, on freedom of speech. Senators are well aware of their favored policy when the time comes to make a choice. The policy preference results from the first four influences working together.

The *Congressional Quarterly* measures of partisanship, ideology, and presidential support indicate that Senators Sarbanes and Lugar are normally poles apart. Yet, at the end of the legislative process, each often supports the other's initiatives. This is the genius of legislation in a democratic assembly, when it puts the national welfare above party advantage.

The legislators finally agree on what to do, even though they may never agree on why it should be done.

The Political Context. The most immediate influence on how someone reacts to an issue is the political context or environment in which the policy preference is weighed. The context is consciously considered at the point of choice. The political environment is all-inclusive, but an obvious component is the senator's position in the Senate, which helps determine the influence he can bring to bear on the issue. Both Sarbanes and Lugar have risen to Senate influence by the traditional route of developing expertise in the subjects of their committees.

But the context never suppresses the prior determinants. The basic ideological difference between Sarbanes and Lugar has been reinforced by different political experiences. One cannot imagine either senator supporting a policy he does not believe in, even if his career should hang in the balance. In each of them, there is an inner core of integrity that remains inviolate. Paradoxically, the fact that reelection is not an all-consuming purpose is probably sensed by many voters and helps to ensure their reelection.

Senate Procedures:
The Triumph of Individualism

Having reached conclusions about the influences affecting the two senators, we now must ask what the careers of these two senators reveal about the nature of the Senate.

While the House of Representatives is organized to debate and then pass legislation, the Senate showcases representation, conceived as the protection of established interests against change. The individual senator has many opportunities to prevent the passage of a law. Any senator can object to the unanimous consent agreement proposed, after careful negotiation, by the Republican and Democratic leaders. Committee chairmen schedule, or refuse to schedule, meetings at their own pleasure. And individuals gaining the floor to filibuster can only be silenced by sixty senators, present and voting.

There is a consensus of thoughtful senators and scholars who study the Senate concerning the nature and impact of institutional change since the 1950s. The old Senate norm of reciprocity prevented senators from using the power available to them under the rules to obstruct Senate progress. The norm is little honored now, and a few senators glory in using those powers. Increased obstructionism is but a symptom of the fragmentation of Senate power into rule by individuals, who are supported by bigger staffs and often place a high value on national publicity. The sense of collegiality that once characterized "the world's most exclusive club" is forgotten. The Senate tends to be a collection of one hundred individualists so lacking in common purpose that they can't agree to discipline the few obstructionists in their ranks.[6]

The public includes the Senate in its generally negative view of the Congress. The five-year average in the *Washington Post*–ABC News poll is 33 percent approval of Congress and 62 percent disapproval. In mid-1994, voters saw the 103rd Congress as "a do-nothing assemblage of quarrelsome partisans more attuned to the special interests than to its constituents."[7]

Aware of public dissatisfaction, the House of Representatives had passed Concurrent Resolution 192 on June 18, 1992, which was joined soon thereafter by the Senate. Thus was formed the Joint Committee on the Organization of Congress, consisting of members from both chambers. Dick Lugar was appointed to membership on the new panel by the Republican leadership; Paul Sarbanes was appointed by the Democratic leadership. Each party appointed five additional members to fill the Senate's quota of twelve seats. By the time decisions were being reached, Bill Clinton had entered the White House.

The Joint Committee's discussion of Senate procedures centered on filibusters and Rule XXII, which provides for cloture. Paul Sarbanes has long favored curbing filibusters, provided the limits apply to all; he does not favor "unilateral disarmament." When he filibustered to protect the Baltimore–Washington airport, Sarbanes carefully avoided general obstruction. Dick Lugar has not participated in a massive, organized filibuster since defeating the labor bill in his first term. Both support the Joint Committee's proposal.

The committee proposed, first, that a motion to consider could be debated no more than two hours. A filibuster could no longer prevent even discussing an issue. Second, any challenge to a ruling by the chair, following a cloture vote, could only be overridden by a three-fifths vote. The extraordinary majority gathered to end a filibuster would no longer find delay renewed by the challenge of a ruling by the chair, which normally requires only a majority of those present. Third, when debate continues under time constraints after cloture, the time consumed by a quorum call would be charged against the time allotted to the person suggesting the absence of a quorum. These changes seem marginal, but their intent was to negate those rules most often used for simple obstruction.

Obstruction is so serious because the Senate is busy with committees clamoring for attention by the full body, the annual budget process, and individual senators gaining the floor to propose floor amendments to bills never considered by their own committees. The Joint Committee formulated a plan for controlling the number of committee assignments held by each member and ways to prevent scheduling conflicts. They also agreed to limit the proliferation of subcommittees. But real reform would require revising the number and jurisdictions of standing committees. This proved impossible, because every senator has a stake, with seniority, in current committee arrangements.

Many critics of Congress saw the source of gridlock not in the body's organization but in its handling of the budget. Each year, Congress goes through a lengthy and complex budgetary process, yet the sums appropriated may vary little from year to year. Fixation on the budget takes the attention of authorizing committees away from legislative oversight, the mechanism for assuring that agencies carry out the law according to congressional intent.

The Joint Committee finally closed ranks behind the proposal for a biennial budget process.[8] Budget resolutions and appropriations bills would cover two years, and program authorizations would extend for at least two years. Stipulating an entirely new, two-year calendar for the budgetary process would ensure that the authorizations were complete before appropriations should begin; this might make the process more understandable, even for ordinary citizens. It would surely give the committees time for other pressing matters.

The details of congressional organization are not of compelling public interest. Activists do not march, nor do talk show hosts agitate, to support a two-year budget cycle. The proposals of the Joint Committee were introduced as legislation but were never acted upon. The initiative was seized in 1995 by House Republicans who, coming into majority status after forty years, claimed to implement the public will. As proprietors of the "Republican Revolution," they had little interest in modest proposals made in the preceding Democratic Congress.

Obstructionism remained. In 1997, Foreign Relations chairman Jesse Helms opposed the nomination of William Weld, a moderate Republican, to be ambassador to Mexico. Weld resigned as governor of Massachusetts to seek confirmation. Helms refused even to hold a hearing on the nomination. Helms was the Senate champion of the tobacco industry; his reason for opposing Weld was that Weld was "soft on drugs," having once supported the medicinal use of marijuana.

Dick Lugar, chairman of the Agriculture Committee, called a press conference to complain that it was time for Helms to realize that the Constitution empowers the entire Senate to "advise and consent" to such nominations, not one committee chairman. Lugar hinted that North Carolina's tobacco interests might not fare very well when tobacco subsidies come before the Agriculture Committee. Later, on *Meet the Press*, Lugar said, "We've really come to a point in the life of the Senate where we really have to have reciprocal relationships that are better."[9] Lugar admitted that he probably wouldn't win Weld's confirmation but confessed that his wider purpose is to force debate on America's posture in the world. The Republican Congressional leadership has little experience, or indeed interest, in international questions. Lugar intends to change that.[10] It seems unlikely that a majority of senators will jointly repudiate their toleration of obstructionism in the Senate.

Extending the Senatorial Life Cycle

After studying the 180 persons who served in the U.S. Senate during the decade after World War II, Donald R. Matthews suggested that there is a senatorial life cycle. The campaign for a second term is crucial; having survived that test, a third-term reelection is very likely. During a third term, the senator is perceived as devoting more attention to national or international issues than to constituent needs. Eighty-eight percent of Matthews' subjects were elected to third terms, but only 57 percent to later terms.[11]

Moving upward through the seniority system, the senator acquired more duties; with them came authority and power. As life in Washington became more absorbing, old friends in the home state passed away, political circumstances changed, and soon the senator was plausibly accused of forgetting the home folks. The chance of winning a fourth or fifth term was less than the chance a freshman had of winning a second term. Matthews noted the irony.

> Not many senators survive to the end of this political life cycle, but for the few who do, defeat suffered at the peak of their careers provides a cruel reminder of their constituents' power.[12]

Lugar and Sarbanes fit the front end of this pattern. Their reelection to second terms was much less certain than their capture of third terms. However, the forces Matthews described did not impede their election to fourth terms.

Travel to the home state does not consume the time or energy required before the jet travel era. Then, senators planned to take one round trip to the home state during each session of Congress. Now, senators may return home nearly every weekend. And the Senate does little crucial business on Mondays or Fridays, so the political weekend may have four effective days. With so many members away, the opportunity for forming friendships barely exists. The habits of civility and compromise have withered.

Senators have methods of communicating with their constituents that were unknown forty years ago. Rather than depending on reporters and newspapers, senators can provide television tapes for local stations, even relaying them by satellite. Tapes may also be supplied to radio stations. These are treated as reports to constituents by their Washington representative, so the stations feel no need to supply equal time for an opposition. Population subgroups may be targeted by "narrowcasting" to the specialized audiences of the different cable television channels. Computers maintain specialized mailing lists and print out form letters on appropriate occasions that seem to result from personal senatorial attention.

In addition to increased capabilities for travel and communication, senators have larger personal staffs. Matthews noted that "the fastest-growing 'bureaucracies' in Washington are found in the Senate Office Building." Typical Senate office staffs consisted of "a dozen or so persons."[13] The trend Matthews spotted continued for at least three decades. Constitution Avenue now boasts a row of three elegant Senate office buildings. By the 1980s, the average Senate staff numbered thirty-one; Matthews' "dozen or so" had nearly tripled. However, staff allotments increase with the size of state populations, so a senator from California or New York could have more than seventy paid assistants.[14]

Senators who use their staff astutely will be able to take on the increased duties that come with seniority, while still keeping in touch with their home state. When chairing a committee, the senator appoints a committee staff which serves at his or her pleasure; the office staff need not be burdened by these new responsibilities.

Finally, it is now far more difficult to challenge an incumbent senator. There are no strong party organizations, even in Indiana, which believe that an incumbent of the opposition party should be challenged, even if firmly entrenched, and are prepared to finance that challenge. Campaign costs have escalated as retail voter contact by party organizations has been replaced by the expensive, wholesale politics of the electronic media. Organized groups with policy interests are the most certain source of funds; incumbents have an enormous advantage in attracting such support. Senators Lugar and Sarbanes are eligible to run for reelection in 2000. Their chances of winning fifth terms seem excellent.

The world and the Senate have changed since Matthews described the senatorial life cycle. The trips home which help make senators impervious to electoral challenge also make the Senate less effective as an institution, by inhibiting the growth of collegiality. Representation perceived as effective by the voters of individual states coexists with the Senate's inability to act on behalf of the nation. With their emphasis on the public good, the Constitution's authors did not intend such irony.

Two Senators and Campaign Finance

The careers of Dick Lugar and Paul Sarbanes span the period of obscene growth in the cost of political campaigning. Think of their campaigns. In 1976, both won against incumbent senators of the opposing party. Each was then in the vanguard of political change in his state, and he was able to finance a winning campaign. As campaign costs have soared, so has the financial advantage enjoyed by incumbents.

The reelection campaigns of Senators Sarbanes and Lugar have been impeccably legal and ethical, but the system has given them enormous advantages. In 1982, when they sought second terms, their challengers suffered from inadequate financial support. Lugar and Sarbanes accepted donations from political action committees but denied that PACs were purchasing undue influence. When they sought third terms in 1988, the opposing parties were barely able to find, much less fund, their opponents. The resulting campaigns were not occasions to ensure informed choice by the electorate; their opponents hardly gained a hearing. However, Paul Sarbanes' campaigns demonstrated that it takes more than money to win elections. In 1994, he was victorious despite being significantly outspent by his opponent.

The public follows much of the press in assuming that members of Congress are more responsive to large contributors than to constituents. However, this dark view of congressional motivation applies only to other people's representatives. The same electorates voting emphatically to limit congressional terms reelect their incumbent members of Congress by equally impressive margins.

For many Americans, the phrase "political action committee" symbolizes unfairly purchased political influence. But a PAC is essentially a way for individuals to pool their funds. "Membership" PACs flourish; they can raise funds from their members (corporations from officers, for example, or unions from members).[15] They can also play the game of making unlimited "independent" contributions to favorite candidates. Independent expenditures by groups ranging from the AFL-CIO through the American Association of Retired Persons to the U.S. Chamber of Commerce in the battle over partisan control of the House of Representatives attained scandalous proportions in 1996.[16]

Organized interests support political candidates in order to influence votes on issues the interests feel are important. Incumbents have published voting records and established leadership positions. When individuals and organizations regard their contributions as investments, they donate to incumbents, for the return is far more predictable. The financial advantage of incumbents results from rational decision-making by contributors.

The only way to ensure something like equal access to campaign funds is to limit private donations and combine spending limits with the provision of public funds. The American public has shown no enthusiasm for allowing tax dollars to be used to support congressional campaigns. Public financing of presidential campaigns is an established fact, but the "checkoff," through which citizens can assign a dollar—recently increased to three—of their taxes to that purpose, is widely ignored. Dick Lugar's campaign for the presidential nomination was set back when there were inadequate government funds to pay all of the matching grant for which he had qualified. The money eventually came, but the delay was painful.

Even a public eager to fund campaigns would confront the U.S. Supreme Court, which has extended the free speech protection of the First Amendment to money. This need not mean that the route to genuine reform lies in amending the Constitution. Patchwork reforms are available which could add up to a qualitative improvement in the system. These include banning "soft money" for the parties, while increasing their ability to raise hard money; providing free television time to parties and qualifying minor party or independent candidates; tax credits for in-state contributions only; and simply assuring adequate funding for the Federal Elections Commission.[17]

No substantial reforms have been made in the campaign finance system since the post-Watergate era. Unless public opinion becomes outraged and mobilized, with strong political leadership, one cannot expect incumbent members of Congress to dismantle the system that so advantages them.

Reflections on the Term Limit Movement

Do the careers of Senators Sarbanes and Lugar shed light on the wisdom of term limitations? When asked about the matter, Dick Lugar said that it would seem ungracious for one who had already served fifteen years to attack the concept, when most versions limit senatorial service to twelve years. Later on in the interview, responding to a different question, he stated that he is assured by their letters that his constituents support him because of believing that their lives are safer with Lugar in the Senate. He was thinking particularly of his successful effort, along with Senator Sam Nunn, to provide financial support for dismantling nuclear weapons by the nations of the former Soviet Union.[18]

Paul Sarbanes' view of his career is stated in less grandiose terms. He speaks of providing high quality representation for the state of Maryland. He would include pork barrel triumphs, such as preserving Maryland's military bases, as well as establishing policies, particularly economic policies, that benefit Marylanders along with the nation.

If Lugar or Sarbanes were barred from further elections to the Senate, the people of their states would be denied the services of able and experienced senators. To deny a certain class of persons eligibility for election limits the right of the people to choose their representatives as certainly as that right would be limited by denying a class of persons the right to vote. Several states attempted to finesse this problem by denying space on the state-printed ballot to incumbents who have served their allotted terms, allowing them to run only as write-in candidates. Daniel Lowenstein of the UCLA law school argues that a simple term limitation and denying ballot space to incumbents are equally unconstitutional. In his view, the exclusive qualifications for Senate membership (thirty years of age, nine years a citizen of the United States, and an inhabitant of the state from which chosen) are stated in Article I of the Constitution. Term limits can be imposed only if the Constitution is amended.[19]

In March 1995, House Republicans failed to pass a term-limitation measure, the only total rejection of an item in their Contract with

America. The 1994 election proved that term limits are not required to achieve a Republican congressional majority; partisan enthusiasm for the concept drained away. However, a substantial part of the electorate exhibits fine bipartisan disdain for all incumbents (except, in practice, their own representatives). The movement for term limits retains momentum, complete with rallies and a lobbying organization.

On May 22, 1995, the U.S. Supreme Court addressed the issue for the first time. By a vote of 5–4, the Court struck down an amendment to the Arkansas Constitution which would have denied space on the ballot to incumbent U.S. senators and representatives after a specified number of terms. The majority opinion followed the arguments of Professor Lowenstein and added that "allowing individual states to craft their own qualifications for Congress would thus erode the structure envisioned by the framers . . . to form 'a more perfect union.'"[20]

The Lessons of Two Senators' Careers

Senators Lugar and Sarbanes won fourth Senate terms, not only because of incumbent advantages, but as representatives of the majority political sentiment of their respective states. First elected in 1976 in the vanguard of political change, by 1994 they personified the political establishment of their states. Establishments are vulnerable to protest, but Dick Lugar and Paul Sarbanes were better equipped—by temperament and technology—than their predecessors to adapt to changes in popular opinion. Furthermore, they established constituent trust that allowed them significant freedom of action.

Their two careers show that we may expect Senate incumbents to retain their seats longer than in the past, if that is their desire. Senator Strom Thurmond is thus a harbinger of the future, although not all senators will desire to serve into their nineties. Should this tendency be curbed by imposing term limits, even at the cost of amending the Constitution? No; in a democracy, the people should be able freely to choose their representatives. The answer is to ensure that their choices will be free by attacking the advantage of incumbents at its source, which is fund-raising. An incumbent who is reelected after a fair contest well deserves to serve.

The campaign finance rules instituted in response to Watergate have run their course. The loopholes have been discovered and enlarged to admit armored cars stuffed with "soft money." At the present writing, attention is focused on the finance of presidential campaigns. Any attempt to preserve the status quo for Congress by avoiding any changes made in presidential practices would be a tragedy. The respect of Americans for their government can only be restored on the basis of certainty that their elected representatives are not for sale.

The authors of the United States Constitution believed that members of the House of Representatives would be particularly close to the voters, giving voice to the changing passions and confusions of the people. The balance wheel of the machine would be the Senate, where cool deliberation could even frustrate the desires of a temporary majority faction.[21] For forty years, the Democratic majority in the House of Representatives seemed increasingly to endure by meeting district needs, rather than responding to changes in the national mood. In 1994, Republican capture of the House of Representatives was hailed as a rebirth of sensitivity to changing national passions, a recovery of the lower chamber's birthright. Paul Sarbanes and Dick Lugar are two senators demonstrably able to carry out Madison's assigned role of cool deliberation. They are also able to lead the Senate in taking initiatives that do not depend on responding to House actions.

Sarbanes and Lugar exemplify the mainstream of senators, dedicated to achieving legislation through orderly committee consideration, accompanied by wide consultation, compromise, and the formation of consensus. Only a few senators consistently exploit the rules to block the legislative process. Unfortunately, the obstructionists largely determine the tone and public image of the Senate. Both Sarbanes and Lugar decry the need for sixty votes—the requirement for cloture—to allow Senate deliberation, because even the motion to discuss a bill may be filibustered.

Every senator can imagine him- or herself someday preventing a determined but misguided majority from taking unwise action. Since senators are ambivalent about majority rule in the Senate, efforts to achieve it are halting and tentative. Both Dick Lugar and Paul Sarbanes, who were members of the Joint Committee on the Organization of Congress, support the reforms proposed by that panel in 1993.

The ordinary process of reasonable disagreement between legislators viewed on C-SPAN television is as likely to foster an image of dullness as one of quarrelsome partisanship. The reality which gives credence to the image of partisanship-run-amok is more likely to transpire on or off the chamber floor in the statements of a Newt Gingrich, David Bonoir, or Richard Armey of the House or, on the Senate side, Jesse Helms, Edward Kennedy, Alfonse D'Amato, Thomas Daschle, Trent Lott, or Phil Gramm.

At some point the reasonable disagreement essential to the legislative process crosses a boundary. It becomes unreasonable disagreement, symbol of an institution in disarray.[22]

The operations of the United States Congress are remarkably complicated. Occasionally a floor vote or a committee hearing attracts extensive media coverage. The stories are presented as if they concerned the only significant congressional activity that day. Yet each issue resolved by Congress marks the formation of a temporary majority formed around that issue alone. And dozens of issues have reached various stages in the process on any given day. However, a single senator can prevent Senate action, while Senate accomplishment requires cooperation. The future of the Senate depends on the extent to which more of their colleagues come to share the attachment of Dick Lugar and Paul Sarbanes to the principles and practices of reasonable disagreement.

Notes

1. See, chapter 6, pp. 88–89.
2. Interview with Senator Lugar, May 26, 1992.
3. Interview, December 16, 1996.
4. Interview with Senator Sarbanes, April 15, 1992.
5. Ibid.
6. See Fred R. Harris, *Deadlock or Decision: The U.S. Senate and the Rise of National Politics* (New York: Oxford University Press, 1993), chapter 4, and the literature cited therein.
7. Richard Morin and David S. Broder, "Familiarity Is Breeding Contempt of Congress," *Washington Post,* July 3, 1994, p. A1.
8. U.S. Congress, Senate, "Final Report of the Joint Committee on the Organization of Congress . . ." Senate Report 103–215, Part 2, December 29, 1993, p. 75.
9. Reuters, "White House Isn't Helping Weld, Lugar Says," *Washington Post,* August 11, 1997, p. A6.
10. Jim Hoagland, "Lugar's Larger Campaign," *Washington Post,* August 14, 1997, p. A21.
11. Donald R. Matthews, *U.S. Senators and Their World* (New York: Vintage Books, 1960), pp. 241–242.
12. Ibid., p. 242.
13. Ibid., p. 82.
14. Roger H. Davidson and Walter J. Oleszek, *Congress and Its Members,* 2d ed. (Washington. D.C.: Congressional Quarterly Press, 1985), p. 245.
15. Sorauf, *Inside Campaign Finance,* pp. 180–181.
16. Jeffrey H. Birnbaum, "Beating the System," *Time,* October 21, 1996, pp. 33–35. Other methods used to skirt the law included giving "soft money" to parties for presumed organizational purposes and "tallying," by which unlimited donations to parties are earmarked to benefit the donor's favorite candidate.

17. These and other promising reforms are discussed in an op-ed essay by Thomas E. Mann and Norman J. Ornstein, "Credibility for a Collapsed System," *Washington Post,* December 16, 1996, p. A25.

18. Interview with Senator Lugar, May 26, 1992.

19. Daniel Hays Lowenstein, "Are Congressional Term Limits Constitutional?" paper prepared for presentation at the annual meeting of the American Political Science Association, 1993. Lowenstein specifically finds "no merit" in the arguments put forth by Roderick M. Hills, Jr., "A Defense of State Constitutional Limits on Federal Congressional Terms," 53 *University of Pittsburgh Law Review* 97 (1991) and Stephen J. Safranek, "Term Limitations: Do the Winds of Change Blow Unconstitutional?" 26 *Creighton Law Review 321* (1993).

20. Majority opinion written by Justice John Paul Stevens in *U.S. Term Limits, Inc. v. Thornton.* Dissenting, Justice Clarence Thomas insisted that "[t]he Constitution is simply silent on this question . . . it raises no bar to action by the States or the people." Opinions excerpted in the *Washington Post,* May 23, 1995, p. A6.

21. See James Madison, *Federalist Papers,* numbers 10 and 51.

22. In *Democracy and Disagreement* (Cambridge: Harvard University Press, 1996), political philosophers Amy Gutmann and Dennis Thompson examine deep disagreement in American democracy and offer "deliberative democracy" as a way for citizens as well as public officials to reason together and come to tolerate, if not resolve, moral disagreements. They define six principles that should constrain democratic decision making. The reasonable disagreement personified by Lugar and Sarbanes in the Senate could be a tentative step toward the reform of social and political processes Gutmann and Thompson recommend.

INDEX